Preaching Adverbially

Preaching Adverbially

F. Russell Mitman

WILLIAM B. EERDMANS PUBLISHING COMPANY
GRAND RAPIDS, MICHIGAN

Wm. B. Eerdmans Publishing Co.
2140 Oak Industrial Drive NE, Grand Rapids, Michigan 49505
www.eerdmans.com

27 26 25 24 23 22 21 20 19 18   1 2 3 4 5 6 7 8 9 10

ISBN 978-0-8028-7558-7

Library of Congress Cataloging-in-Publication Data

Names: Mitman, F. Russell, author.
Title: Preaching adverbially / F. Russell Mitman.
Description: Grand Rapids : Eerdmans Publishing Co., 2018. |
    Includes bibliographical references and index.
Identifiers: LCCN 2017025508 | ISBN 9780802875587 (pbk. : alk. paper)
Subjects: LCSH: Preaching.
Classification: LCC BV4211.3 .M585 2018 | DDC 251—dc23
    LC record available at https://lccn.loc.gov/2017025508

To Norman A. Hjelm,
mentor and friend

Contents

Foreword

At several points in the succession of essays on preaching that fill this book, Russell Mitman refers to the altarpiece that Lucas Cranach painted in 1547 for the City Church—St. Mary's Church—in Wittenberg, Germany, the very church where Martin Luther himself had been pastor. That altarpiece images baptism, the Lord's Supper, and confession and forgiveness as events that occur in and give identity to the assembly that met and still meets in this church. Underneath these sacramental images and just above the altar itself, Cranach also painted an image for preaching: Luther is using the biblical text to point toward the crucified Christ, and the assembly of local people find their life in that same cross. Indeed, the whole altarpiece finds its center in the cross, and the room is then filled with a wind of the Spirit—represented by the billowing loincloth of the Crucified—that blows from the cross toward the preacher, toward the painted assembly, and toward us.

Something of that same life-giving wind blows here, in these pages. These essays also locate preaching in the midst of the assembly, surrounded by the sacraments, filled with the presence of Christ, listening to the Bible, set very near the Lord's Table. Pastor Mitman is right that preaching in our time often lacks clarity of purpose. He is also right that sermons can be inserted within worship services as if they have nothing much to do with the whole communal event, as if they are a separate sort of thing. Not in the Cranach altarpiece. And not in these essays. Mitman's adverbs help us see the whole of worship as an event of proclamation, "gospeling," as he says, giving preference to a verbal form. And the adverbial refreshment with which he modifies that verb gives a new depth of vocation to the preacher in the midst of the liturgy, a vocation very like that of Luther in the St. Mary's Church image.

It is a gift to look again at this Luther-related image in this year commemorating the 500th anniversary of the Reformation. More: it is a gift to think of preaching as a communal and sacramental undertaking, with the preacher playing one important and integral role but not doing everything. It is also a gift to do this thinking ecumenically, with Pastor Mitman as guide. He is himself, by vocation, a preacher. He has also been a pastor and bishop to preachers and their assemblies, a "conference minister," as the United Church of Christ says, an *episcopos*, a supervisor or overseer, as the old church tradition would have it. And he has been in endless conversations about preaching. Those conversations—with other pastors and congregation members, with scholars and writers, with his teachers and his students, with the very structure of the Revised Common Lectionary—yield fruit here. The very fact that both Luther and Karl Barth are found cogently present in these pages testifies to the remarkable Reformed-Lutheran background of Mitman's own Mercersburg tradition, with its strong accent on both preaching and the sacraments. But Orthodox, Episcopalian, Roman Catholic, and yet other Protestant voices are found here as well. The book is a conversation, and I believe that you are welcome to join it.

Let the gospeling word of preaching faithfully use the Bible and its metaphors, responsibly correspond to the context, compellingly invite to the sacramental actions, accurately tell the truth about our need and God's mercy—to use only a few of the adverbs implied here. And so let it blow with that life-giving wind from the cross.

GORDON W. LATHROP

Acknowledgments

I am deeply grateful for the many opportunities I have had to put in praxis what I am proposing in the following chapters. I thank the many church leaders, lay and clergy, in a variety of settings across the ecumenical spectrum who have invited me into their assemblies and who have provided support and critical reflection as these chapters have unfolded. I am grateful to the staff of Wm. B. Eerdmans Publishing Company for their willingness to take on this project and to guide it to fruition. And, of course, I am thankful to my family and friends who have cheered me on for nearly five years as this book has taken shape. My hope is that this book's eleven chapters can become catalysts to inspire worship leaders to become immersed in the homiletical and liturgical arts for the upbuilding of the body of Christ.

F. RUSSELL MITMAN
PENTECOST, 2017

Introduction

And how shall they hear without a preacher?

—Romans 10:14 KJV

The question may be asked justifiably: Why another book on preaching? Fred Craddock's monumental 1985 work, *Preaching*,[1] had everything that needs to be known about preaching. Furthermore, in the generation since Craddock's work many shelves of books on preaching and electronic libraries full of texts and visuals have been produced. Why another book on preaching?

When I was doing graduate work in preaching, one of the assigned texts was an anthology on the shaping of sermons by Don Wardlaw titled *Preaching Biblically*.[2] The book contained essays and sample sermons by Wardlaw and other professors of preaching, some of whom were my own mentors and teachers. Then there are a whole host of others who have helped shape my homiletical practice—professors, preachers, and people in the pews. Every year when I sing Handel's *Messiah* and the chorus based on Psalm 68:11, "Great Was the Company of the

1. Fred B. Craddock, *Preaching* (Nashville: Abingdon, 1985).
2. Don M. Wardlaw, ed., *Preaching Biblically: Creating Sermons in the Shape of Scripture* (Philadelphia: Westminster, 1983).

1

Preachers," I am reminded of this "great company of preach-ers" who have accompanied me on my half-century preaching journey. In Handel's musical setting of the psalm-verse, the text is belted out by basses and tenors. Yet, it is a corrective to add that in the Psalm the "great company" are women! As Today's New International Version translates Psalm 68:11: "The Lord an-nounces the word, and the women who proclaim it are a mighty throng." I like to quote that translation from time to time!

Wardlaw's *Preaching Biblically*, and particularly its subtitle, *Creating Sermons in the Shape of Scripture*, provided impetus for my own reflections on creating liturgical expressions that resulted in *Worship in the Shape of Scripture*.[3] The claim of that volume is to forward the suggestion that the same hermeneutic involved in the creation of a sermon is also operative in the crafting of liturgy. And both sermon and liturgy aim together at an engage-ment with the Word of God.

All along, Wardlaw's adverb "biblically" kept sticking in my mind and has raised questions about other adverbs asso-ciated with the art of preaching. What has emerged out of my own experience as a preacher in a variety of settings and from having been in the presence of great preaching and great preachers is this collection of reflections, *Preaching Adverbially*. In most cases, the adverbs are dictionary-found. Two had to be coined with an -*ly* affixed. My hope is that these chapters are complementary sequels focusing, from the perspective of the homiletical arts, on the ideas I first proposed in *Worship in the Shape of Scripture*, namely that homiletics and liturgics are mar-ried arts, and that the whole worship service is a unified act of preaching the Word of God. So, the reader may wonder from time to time throughout these chapters: Is this about preaching sermons, or is it about doing liturgy? It is about both. Liturgics and homiletics cannot be separated. They are married arts, and assemblies all preach each time they gather in their singing and speaking, praying and proclaiming, eating and drinking,

3. F. Russell Mitman, *Worship in the Shape of Scripture* (Cleveland: Pil-grim, 2001, 2009).

blessing and baptizing. Preaching is sermons, but much more. Preaching is what assemblies do whenever they worship God. My goal in these reflections is to try to rescue "preaching" from the narrows of "sermonizing."

The reader may ask, "Why the adverbs? Why the *-ly* words?" Grammatically, adverbs are different from adjectives. Much has been written about various kinds or styles of preaching—"preaching" prefixed with adjectives such as "biblical preaching," "sacramental preaching," and so on. Rarely, however, do we find books and articles on preaching in adverbs, which shift the meaning from a description of the "thing," preaching, that is, to the action of doing the preaching and what *happens* in the doing. Therefore, what I hope in the next eleven chapters is to explore what happens in the art of preaching adverbially, and in doing so, I also hope to be teaching what I consider are the central issues in worship.

Traditionally the academic discipline in seminaries in which the teaching of preaching is lodged is/was called "homiletics," and in some ecclesial traditions sermons are therefore called "homilies." The root of all these words is the Greek word *homilos*, which is translated literally as "crowd." Homiletics presupposed a crowd, a gathering of people, an assembly, who will be engaged in a *homilia*, a conversation—not just any old chitchat, but an intentional conversation with God—not just about God, but with God—and with the people of God. And when assemblies are engaged in conversations with God and one another, the discipline of doing that is called liturgics, from the Greek *leitourgia*, which simply means "work" in the sense of "public service." When associated with worship, liturgics has to do with the doing of worship. Both homiletics and liturgics are wedded in the praxis of worshiping God, and both aim simultaneously at preaching the Word of God in the context of an assembly gathered with the focused intent of doing its worship work. So this book argues that there is one Word, Jesus Christ, who is proclaimed and who is present in an assembly through the Holy Spirit in the actions of Word and Sacrament; that preaching is more than a sermon and is the intent of the whole liturgical action (*ordo*); and that this action is best captured in adverbs that constitute the themes of the following chapters, beginning with the Bible and progressing through to the eschaton.

Chapter 1 discusses what it means to preach *biblically*. An assembly is encountered by the Word of God through the Holy Scriptures as Word-event; the hermeneutic for this action is what Luke records in Jesus's first sermon: "Today this scripture has been fulfilled in your hearing"; and the whole of the homiletical/liturgical event is ordered by the biblical texts themselves.

Chapter 2, on preaching *liturgically*, aims at expanding "preaching" to encompass the whole of the liturgical event; to show how each worship expression, including the sermon, is part of an organic whole shaped by the biblical texts; and to demonstrate that all of worship is a preaching event.

So also we aim at preaching *sacramentally* (chapter 3). For half a millennium, what constitutes a sacrament and how many sacraments there are has been an unfinished debate and a source of division in the church. This chapter explores the integral and inseparable connection between preaching and sacraments and claims there is a fundamental difference between sacramental preaching and preaching sacramentally.

"Evangelical preaching" has become co-opted by certain brands of American religion and reduced to a means of making converts. Chapter 4 aims to free preaching *evangelically* from these restrictive and even pejorative associations; to explore the New Testament *euangelion* (gospel) as more than a noun or adjective but as a verb; and to suggest that preaching evangelically is "gospel-ing," letting the Word of God happen in grace and judgment in the midst of an assembly.

To preach *contextually* (chapter 5) intends to explore the ways, through preaching and worship, the Word of God witnessed to in the Scriptures seeks embodiment in the various social and political contexts in which assemblies find themselves. This chapter aims at exploring the deeper issue of allowing the biblical texts to recontextualize themselves in the act of re-oralizing the texts in the worship event, so that the focus is not on what happened then, but on what God is doing now.

Preaching evangelically is inviting people into what lies between the "already" and the "not yet." So we preach *invitationally* (chapter 6), moving beyond imparting of information or even persuading to a gospeling that invites people into a mystery greater than themselves. Preaching invitationally means enticing the assembly into the living Word of God, Jesus Christ.

To preach *metaphorically* (chapter 7) involves allowing the rich metaphors throughout the Bible to actualize themselves homiletically and liturgically in the life of assemblies. Metaphors "carry over" assemblies from what is everyday experience into mysteries and meanings beyond the words themselves—without the necessity to explain or provide theological and doctrinal rationales.

Whereas much of Protestant preaching has been restricted to hearing words spoken and sung, preaching *multisensorily* (chapter 8) explores engaging all five senses—visually, tastably, olfactorily, tactually, as well as auditorily. An integrated approach to preaching through liturgy and sermon allows for an assembly's multisensory engagement with the Word of God.

Chapter 9 explores the difference between "engaging preaching" based on performance theories and the art of preaching *engagingly* within the more encompassing doing of the whole liturgy engagingly. In the former, worship leaders, including preachers, become performers, and the assembly is relegated to being a passive audience. Preaching engagingly involves the whole assembly gospeling engagingly.

The theological ends of preaching are the glorification of God and anticipation of the ultimate fulfillment of the gospel. In contrast to what is often attempted to "contemporize" seemingly boring and uninspiring liturgies and sermons, preaching *doxologically* (chapter 10) is premised on allowing the intrinsic joy of the gospel to be articulated and enacted homiletically and liturgically.

Much has been said and written about "eschatological preaching," yet to entertain the idea that preaching is itself eschatologically oriented and itself an eschatological event pushes "eschatology" into the adverbial. Preaching *eschatologically* is enabling an assembly to participate in the already-but-not-yet-ness of the word of God. Preaching eschatologically seeks to rescue worship and sermons from literalistic predictions of the end-time and to free preachers and presiders to gospel both the promise and fulfillment of living in these in-between times.

I see what follows as personal reflections on the art of preaching. My style is more homiletical and liturgical than academic and didactic, hopefully more pastoral than professorial. Along the way I will share some of the thoughts of those in the great company of preachers who have been my mentors on my journey and the shapers of my praxis. The chapters can be viewed as individual treatises, yet there is an intrinsic movement from preaching biblically to preaching eschatologically. I invite the reader to come along with me in this exploration of preaching adverbially.

* * *

Fred Craddock remarked thirty years ago that he was happy to have lived long enough to see a renaissance in preaching. He along with a great company of preachers and a whole host of nonclergy types rescued the homiletical arts from a perceived irrelevancy. Paul's question, "And how shall they hear without a preacher?," first raised in the first century, raises itself with crucial urgency in the twenty-first century when the church of Jesus Christ finds itself again in the same kind of cultural environment of secularism, hedonism, idolatry, and even persecution. There is an aphorism that the church is always but one generation away from extinction, and Paul's question takes on a compelling contemporaneity. Thank God for a great company of preachers who dare to preach in order that the world may hear what God is saying and doing. And thank God that there are those—many under age thirty—who desire to have ears to hear and to do the gospel in the living of these days.

1

*Preaching **Biblically***

"Today this scripture has been fulfilled in your hearing."

—Luke 4:21

Wardlaw's anthology, *Preaching Biblically: Creating Sermons in the Shape of Scripture*, provides the title and perspective of this chapter. "But *must* I preach on a biblical text?" was overheard in a class in homiletics. And the tone was more of defiance than of query. Yet, there is a certain legitimacy in that question. Is a sermon without basis in a biblical text a sermon?

A presumption behind the student's question is that a sermon, over the centuries of the Christian experience, has been perceived essentially as a rational argument. In his introduction to *Preaching Biblically* Wardlaw says, "For most preachers in the Western tradition . . . preaching, per se, has meant marshaling an argument in logical sequence, coordinating and subordinating points by the canons of logic, all in a careful appeal to the reasonable hearer." He goes on, "To use Tom Long's image, . . . argument has served as the mold into which the gelatin of sermon content was invariably poured."[1] One well-seasoned pastor and preacher many years ago summarized to me the

1. Don M. Wardlaw, ed., *Preaching Biblically* (Philadelphia: Westminster, 1983), 12.

way in which he was taught to preach: "Three points and a poem." The mandatory three points were the meat; the poem was added for taste appeal. Many of us started our own preaching careers in the three-point-and-a-poem paradigm, and sadly, the rigidity of sermon "points" still persists. My retort has been that a sermon is essentially pointless! Of course, that kind of rhetoric begs further elucidation!

Based on Wardlaw's diagnosis that the traditional premise for preaching was rational argument, then the student asking the sermon-question could, in such an understanding of preaching, come up with a rational argument about something religious and put together three points, and maybe a poem, that, in some quarters, might pass for a sermon. Yet the question still stands: What is the difference between a sermon and a speech, between preaching and lecturing?

There's many a church website or church sign publicizing "Sound Biblical Preaching," or, "We Preach the Bible," or, "Bible-Based Sermons." Such advertising gimmicks, to me, are simply code words for various shades of biblical fundamentalism in which preaching is still an argument proof-texted with a smattering of scriptural snippets to prove the preacher's argument—often based more on cultural ideologies than biblical and historical theology.

Therefore, in my understanding, there is a vast difference between *biblical* preaching and preaching *biblically*, a difference between the adjective and the adverb. In his 1969 book, *As One without Authority*,[2] Fred Craddock broke the sermon's gelatin mold, and in the last almost fifty years has changed the way we approach preaching. It has often been said that a good sermon engages the biblical text, as though there is some preconceived idea that looks to the biblical text for validation, yet my premise is the reverse: *the biblical text engages the sermon.* And the metaphor—which I hope is not too prosaic—is of the gearbox in my car in which the engine is engaged to the driving wheels. The biblical text drives the sermon. Action, as in an

2. Fred B. Craddock, *As One without Authority* (St. Louis: Chalice, 1969).

adverb, is intended in preaching biblically. The Word of God is an action-event in which the biblical text is not an add-on or sidebar. Proclamation of the Word is driven by the biblical texts that themselves were driven and still are driven by the Word of God. More on that later. And, as Craddock and many more since then have taught, the biblical text not only *drives* the sermon but provides the homiletical *form* the sermon takes. Preaching biblically is a matter of allowing the scriptural texts to shape the preaching event.

I have always affirmed that the homiletical arts are more akin to the musical arts than to the canons of rational argument. Therefore, borrowing a term from the catalogue of musical disciplines, I maintain that interpreting biblical texts homiletically involves the art of transposition. Paul Wilson writes, "In music, transposing involves writing or playing in a different key from the one designated in the musical score. [In preparing a sermon], we are similarly after a change of key. . . . The tune must be the same since the . . . sermon/homily can only derive its authority from the text."[3] Thus the question with which the preacher/homilist approaches the crafting of a sermon according to Thomas Long is: "How may the sermon, in a new setting, say and do what the text says and does in its setting?"[4] Perhaps a further refinement would be: "How may the sermon, in a new setting, *be* and do what the text is and does in its setting?" In the words of Paul Ricoeur, "The text must be able . . . to 'decontextualize' itself in such a way that it can be 'recontextualized' in a new situation."[5] The New Testament is full of recontextualizations of the Old Testament, and some

---

3. Paul Scott Wilson, *Imagination of the Heart: New Understandings of Preaching* (Nashville: Abingdon, 1988), 86.

4. Thomas G. Long, *Preaching and the Literary Forms of the Bible* (Philadelphia: Fortress, 1989), 33. (As of this writing Long's classic is still in print and even available on Kindle!)

5. Paul Ricoeur, "The Hermeneutical Function of Distanciation," in *Hermeneutics and the Social Sciences*, ed. and trans. John B. Thompson (Cambridge: Cambridge University Press, 1981), 139, quoted in Long, *Preaching and the Literary Forms of the Bible*, 35.

very interesting things happen when a text originally written—
and in some cases even passed on orally as in the Psalms—in
Hebrew is recontextualized in Koine Greek. I pause to ask the
initial question of this chapter again—rhetorically, "Is a sermon
without a text a sermon?"

Many years ago I had the privilege of participating in
seminars conducted by Gerhard Ebeling of the University of
Tübingen in Germany. The first English-translation edition of
his *Word and Faith* had appeared in 1963. (*Word and Faith* was
released in a new edition in 2012, nearly fifty years after its
first appearance!) During the readings for those seminars I underlined some words of *Word and Faith*, and even now the book
wants to fall open to these lines: "Whatever precise theological
definition may be given to the concept of the Word of God, at
all events it points us to something that happens. . . ."[6] The
verb "to happen" in German is *geschehen*, and in the noun form
Geschehen is translated as "event."

Ebeling's sentence goes on, and my underlining continues:
". . . *viz.* to the movement which leads from the text of holy
scripture to the sermon ('sermon' of course taken in the pregnant sense of proclamation in general)."[7] Something happens
in that movement from the text of holy Scripture to whatever
mode of proclamation in the worship event becomes a vessel
through which the Word of God is experienced. Understanding
again that his use of *Predigt* in German (translated in English as
"sermon") refers literally to "that which is preached," we listen
in again to Ebeling: "The process from text to sermon can . . .
be characterized by saying: proclamation that has taken place is
to become proclamation that takes place. This transition from
text to sermon is a transition from scripture to the spoken word.
Thus the task . . . consists in making what is written into spoken
word or . . . in letting the text become God's Word again."[8]

6. Gerhard Ebeling, *Word and Faith*, trans. James W. Leitch (Philadelphia: Fortress, 1963), 311.

7. Ebeling, *Word and Faith*, 311.

8. Ebeling, *Word and Faith*, 329.

That task of letting the text become God's Word again involves what came to be known as the "hermeneutical circle," first suggested by Friedrich Schleiermacher in the nineteenth century and developed by philosopher Martin Heidegger in 1927. Yet, much earlier than the theses of German theologians and philosophers, a hermeneutical circle is found in Scripture itself. In the account in Luke 4 of Jesus's visit to the synagogue in Nazareth, Jesus was given the scroll of the prophet Isaiah, and he read the passage from Isaiah 61:1–2a, "The Spirit of the Lord is upon me. . . ." And then, Luke says, he "rolled up the scroll, gave it back to the attendant, and sat down. The eyes of all in the synagogue were fixed on him. Then he began to say to them, 'Today this scripture has been fulfilled in your hearing' [literally 'in your ears']" (Luke 4:20–21). Here in one sentence we have a description of the Bible's own hermeneutical circle. "Today," in this moment in history, "this scripture," an ancient text witnessing to the Word of God, "has been fulfilled in your hearing," as the Word of God is enfleshed in that assembly's participation in Jesus's proclamation.

In some liturgical traditions, there is a significant preface to the reading of Scripture and the preaching of the sermon that is referred to as the prayer or collect for illumination. We find evidence in the rubrics of Martin Bucer's *The Strassburg Liturgy* (1539) and in John Calvin's *The Form of Church Prayers* (Strassburg, 1545; Geneva, 1542). The rubrics in Bucer's liturgy state:

> When the singing is over [a Psalm, that is], the Minister offers a short prayer for grace and a right spirit, that the Sermon and Word of God which are to follow may be heard with profit. The prayer is to this effect:
>
> > The Lord be with you.
> > Let us pray.
>
> Almighty gracious Father, forasmuch as our whole salvation depends upon our true understanding of thy holy Word, grant to all of us that our hearts, being freed from worldly affairs, may hear and apprehend thy holy Word with all diligence and faith, that we may rightly understand thy gracious

will, cherish it, and live by it with all earnestness, to thy praise and honor; through our Lord Jesus Christ. Amen.[9]

The rubrics in Calvin's Geneva liturgy state: "Then [after the singing of a Psalm] the Minister commences again to pray, beseeching God for the grace of His Holy Spirit, that His Word may be faithfully expounded to the honor of His name and the edification of the Church, and be received with such humility and obedience which it deserves. The form is left to the discretion of the Minister."[10]

The "prayer or collect for illumination" becomes the introduction to the "Word" portion of the worship service and focuses the liturgical action on what will follow—namely the reading of Scripture and the preaching of a sermon. Note also that the rubrics in the selections above treat the reading of Scripture and the preaching as an integrated whole of which the prayer for illumination is the epicletic preparation. In my mind, a prayer for illumination is a far more grace-full and humble approach than a sometimes arrogantly intoned, "May the words of my mouth and the meditation of my heart be acceptable to you, O Lord, my rock and my redeemer" from Psalm 19:14 at the beginning of the sermon. More on that later.

In the recently published *Glory to God* hymnal of the Presbyterian Church USA, the liturgy for the Lord's Day includes this prayer for illumination:

> Lord, open our hearts and minds
> by the power of your Holy Spirit,
> that as the Scriptures are read
> and your Word is proclaimed,
> we may hear with joy
> what you say to us today. Amen.[11]

9. Bard Thompson, ed., *Liturgies of the Western Church* (Cleveland: World, 1961), 170–71.

10. Thompson, ed., *Liturgies of the Western Church*, 198–99.

11. *Glory to God* (Louisville: Westminster John Knox, 2013), 5.

Of particular note in this prayer is that the power of the Holy Spirit is invoked to illuminate not only the reading and hearing of the Word in Scripture but also the reception by the assembly of the Word proclaimed in sermon, homily, or whatever homiletical mode of proclamation is employed. In orders of worship that I have crafted, the lectors and/or assemblies always pray the prayer for illumination *before* the reading of the Scriptures, each one of which is followed by: "Listen for the Word of God." This both preserves the unity of Scripture and proclamation as a single Word act.

Moreover, a prayer of illumination, of which the above is a fine example, as indicated in the introduction to *Book of Common Worship*, "seeks the illumination of the Holy Spirit and calls upon God to make us receptive to the life-giving Word, which comes to us through the Scripture."[12] Also, to quote again from the introductory chapter of *Book of Common Worship*, "When the Bible has been read, its message is proclaimed in a sermon or other form of exposition of God's Word. The God who speaks in Scripture speaks to us now. The God who acted in biblical history acts *today*. Through the Holy Spirit, Christ is present in the sermon, offering grace and calling for obedience. The Word may also be proclaimed through music and other art forms faithful to the gospel."[13] In other words, the Word act in its organic unity is, together with the sacraments of baptism and holy communion, a means of grace. The Word of God happens today in Christian assembly through the "powerful benediction of the Holy Spirit," to lift a phrase from the so-called "Mercersburg" liturgy of 1866. And we "hear"—of course that is metaphoric language—what God is "saying" to us *now*. "It will be true," Barbara Brown Taylor affirms, "not at the level of explanation but at the level of experience. . . . There is another way to preach in which the preacher addresses the congregation not as mute students, but as active partners in the process of

12. *Book of Common Worship* (Louisville: Westminster John Knox, 1993), 36.

13. *Book of Common Worship*, 37.

discovering God's word. . . . The movement of the sermon . . . finally leads both preacher and congregation into the presence of God, a place that cannot be explained but only experienced."[14]

What looks at me from the above-the-desk bookcase where a number of hymnals, psalters, and books of liturgical resources—including the Bible!—are found is a reproduction of the altarpiece in the Stadtkirche St. Marien in Wittenberg, Germany, where Martin Luther preached. It was painted in 1547 by one of Luther's fans, Lucas Cranach the Elder. The large triptych on the upper level depicts the administration of the sacraments: baptism (left panel), holy communion (middle panel), and confession (right panel). The base painting's setting is a building with a floor and two side walls, presumably of a church. On the left is an assembly that includes supposedly Luther's wife, Katharina von Bora, and other family members. On the right wall there is a pulpit in which Luther is preaching. His left index finger points to words in the Bible opened on the pulpit. His right hand points, with the traditional Latin benediction gesture, to the center of the painting. There is a cross, arising from the floor, with the corpus of Christ wrapped around the waist by a white cloth (shroud?).

Cranach's masterpiece illustrates what happens in preaching. Luther, using these symbolic gestures, is preaching. The text is open before him, and his one hand points to the text. The assembly is gathered to hear the Word of God. And when Luther gestures toward the center, the cross becomes central, and the assembly "sees"—I believe in Johannine language—the crucified Christ. And the words of Luke 4:21 are recontextualized: "Today this scripture is fulfilled in your hearing." The fluttering white wrapping around Christ's waist has always captivated me. What did Cranach intend? The setting for the preaching moment is not out of doors. There's no wind that seems to be blowing, although medieval churches are, indeed, drafty! Could it be that the wind of the Holy Spirit is

14. Barbara Brown Taylor, *The Preaching Life* (Cambridge, MA: Cowley, 1993), 82–83.

Lucas Cranach the Elder, Altarpiece, Stadtkirche St. Marien, Wittenberg, Germany, 1547

blowing in an epicletic moment in which the assembly finds the crucified and risen Word made present in the reading and preaching?

Preaching biblically, as illustrated so well in Luke's account of Jesus's one-sentence homily in the synagogue in Nazareth and portrayed graphically in Cranach's altarpiece, involves the hermeneutic of oralizing and re-oralizing. "Today this scripture [written text] has been fulfilled in your hearing" [literally, "in your ears"]. The text of Isaiah 61:1–2a that was given him was in manuscript form—Hebrew words inscribed on parchment. Jesus's reading of the text aloud in the context of an assembly was an act of oralizing, allowing the written text to be recontextualized in an oral (Jesus speaking) and aural (the assembly hearing) event. According to Luke, the fulfillment—that is the meaning—of the text occurred in the assembly's experience. Further, every time that same text is read aloud again in a Christian assembly, it is being re-oralized in yet another context and aims at being a new word-event happening in that particular place and time. Three different readers, for example, oralizing the same biblical text will bring with each reading three nuanced interpretations. "The condition of words in a text," wrote the late Walter Ong, "is quite different from their condition in spoken discourse."[15] "God is thought of always as 'speaking' to human beings, not as writing to them. . . . The Hebrew *dabar* which means word, means also event and thus refers directly to the spoken word. The spoken word is always an event, a movement in time, completely lacking the thing-like repose of the written or printed word."[16] To provide the words of each Sunday's lections printed for those in the assembly to "read along" with the lector or preacher, to me, militates against the orality of the word-event, especially when the lector mispronounces "Nebuchadnezzar"! The same can be said regarding "pew Bibles" to which lectors refer the assembly: "Please turn to page ___ in the New Testament section." Leaflets and bulletin inserts may be available for the hearing-impaired, and some churches enable persons who are deaf to "hear" through the medium of American sign language. Moreover, "hearing" biblically and homiletically is always more than can be heard, even by those who have ears to hear!

Likewise, moving from a sermon spoken to a sermon printed relegates what is intended to become part of an oral and aural event to what Ong described as a "thing-like repose." I prepare a full manuscript for each sermon, and then I reformat the text into a printed folder for those who desire to read the words again or to pass the sermon on to someone else. However, the manuscript is prepared for speaking, and what is meant for *speaking* falls flat in literary form like a left-over fizzy soda. A sermon denuded of its liturgical and corporate setting in an assembly begs the question as to whether it really should be called a "sermon" at all. And even though a sermon can be captured electronically by the most sophisticated devices and technical experts and even broadcast for distant or later reception, without the "live" moment of an assembly gathered by, with, and under the word, it still sinks into a "thing-like repose."

After a many-year hiatus in weekly preaching in the same congregation, I have the privilege again to be approached by

15. Walter J. Ong, *Orality and Literacy* (London: Routledge, 1988), 101.
16. Ong, *Orality and Literacy*, 75.

texts that seek homiletical recontextualizing each Sunday. As of this writing I have reached a six-year anniversary in the congregation I am serving, and the texts of the Revised Common Lectionary have now repeated themselves twice. Since I store all sermons in an electronic "barrel," it is sometimes tempting to look back at what I preached three years ago. Yet, again, there is a certain staleness that accrues in the barrel and renders a repeat of a former edition homiletically useless and maybe even unethical. It's an embarrassment to the preacher for someone who heard that sermon in its previous incarnation to whisper to the person sitting next to her, "He said all that before!" "Overhearing the Gospel," to use the title of a wonderful book by Fred Craddock,[17] is much more than rehearing the same sermon preached three years before, and maybe three years before that, as though folks don't remember! The "shelf-life" of a sermon rarely extends beyond that Sunday's benediction.

Am I a slave to the lectionary? Yes, most often, for to practice and to honor the homiletical arts I—and the congregation I serve—need to be encountered by texts that are not of our own choosing. Again, the difference between preaching biblically and so-called biblical preaching is allowing the texts to encounter us rather than going back to the Bible and searching for what suits the thematic moment—particularly the secular and commercial calendars: Mother's Day, Father's Day, Children's Day, Grandparents' Day, Memorial Day, Independence Day, Veterans' Day, or even for some sermon series based on biblical themes. There's a thematic day possible for fifty-two Sundays—and there are many possible texts to choose from in the Bible to fit fifty-two themes. But keeping the lectionary keeps me from my pet peeves and my pet texts. Barbara Brown Taylor has said:

> I have been a lectionary preacher for so long that I fumble when I have to pick a text out of thin air for a special occa-

17. Fred B. Craddock, *Overhearing the Gospel: Preaching and Teaching the Faith to Persons Who Have Heard It All Before* (Nashville: Abingdon, 1978).

sion. When I pick the text, it seems that I am shopping for a piece of scripture that will back up what I already know I want to say. When the text picks me, I know I am in for a discovery. The lectionary provides me with breadth and discipline I lack on my own, and my sermons are fresher with it than without it. The liturgical year provides a natural pattern for preaching.[18]

When I began my homiletical praxis many years ago, following a lectionary was more the exception than the norm. However, in the intervening years in mainline churches the Revised Common Lectionary has become more and more determinative in the shaping of worship. Moreover, some recently published hymnals even include an index of hymns for each Sunday in the three-year lectionary cycle—proving that the singing of hymns is part of the total proclamatory event. Some lectionary websites provide suggested hymns appropriate to each of the scriptural texts and links to other websites that provide hymn texts and music. And Christian education resources have been created around the lectionary cycle with the intention of integrating worship and Christian formation. There are significant discussions—pro and con—regarding the use of a lectionary, the Revised Common Lectionary in particular, and I need to provide the caveat that any lectionary itself is not the gospel. Nor is any other outline for the systematic reading of Scripture in worship, including the *lectio continuo*, book-by-book, chapter-by-chapter, verse-by-verse approach, favored by some early Reformed reformers, an end in itself.

It has been the practice in the churches I have served to gather midweek Bible study groups to read and study together the texts for the next Sunday's worship. I once led a worship field trip to the National Cathedral in Washington, DC. As the lector there announced the first reading for that Sunday, one of the participants in the field trip who also regularly attended

---

18. From Thomas G. Long, "Patterns in Sermons," in *Best Advice for Preaching*, ed. John S. McClure (Minneapolis: Fortress, 1998), 41.

the midweek Bible study sessions leaned over to me somewhat astonished and whispered in my ear, "That's the same lesson we studied on Tuesday!" She got it that one purpose of churches all being addressed by the same texts each Sunday regardless of geography or denominational label celebrates the unity of the church that is inherent in the body of Christ. Although there will be a huge diversity in the ways in which a particular Sunday's lections are recontextualized in churches across the denominational spectrum, there is an inherent theological perspective that underlies them all. Christ is one, and the ecumenical agenda is not for us to try to *create* Christian unity. What binds us together already has been accomplished in Christ and witnessed to in the gospel—a gospel that comes to us in and through the biblical texts. So, for me to assume that I as preacher have the liberty to put aside the texts through which, by ecumenical consensus, other Christians will encounter the Word, is almost arrogant and factious.

The other affirmation of the whisper in my ear in the National Cathedral echoes what Gail Ramshaw says in her treatise on the lectionary, *A Three-Year Banquet: The Lectionary for the Assembly*: "The gospel is among us because Christ's word speaks by the Spirit to and through us all. . . . God's word is not the private property of the clergy, but is known and treasured by all the people of God. If we know the readings each week, we accompany the preacher into the sermon."[19]

Yesterday I was introduced to a person who was present in a worshiping assembly in which both he and I were strangers to each other. Whether or not he was a "clergy type" I do not know. He said, in essence, "I was a [denominational label withheld] and I never knew anything about the lectionary. But, since I have been part of this church and each week I hear readings from the Old Testament, Epistles, and Gospels, plus a Psalm, I am drawn into the whole sweep of the Bible throughout the whole cycle of the church year." It was a remarkable testimony

---

19. Gail Ramshaw, *A Three-Year Banquet: The Lectionary for the Assembly* (Minneapolis: Augsburg Fortress, 2004), 13.

of an individual who has experienced what can happen in an encounter with the Scriptures liturgically and homiletically through the discipline of the lectionary.

Preaching biblically, I affirm, is the homiletical praxis of inviting the assembly to accompany the preacher, through biblical texts, into an event that is intended to become for the assembly the Word of God through the Holy Spirit. So, preaching biblically, to stretch Gail Ramshaw's metaphor, invites us into a wonder-full and grace-filled banquet in which Christ the one Word of God is present and meets us in Word and Sacrament.

2

Preaching **Liturgically**

For what we preach is not ourselves, but Jesus Christ as Lord, with ourselves as your servants for Jesus' sake. For it is the God who said, "Let light shine out of darkness," who has shone in our hearts to give the light of the knowledge of the glory of God in the face of Christ. But we have this treasure in earthen vessels, to show that the transcendent power belongs to God and not to us.

—2 Corinthians 4:5–7 RSV

Decades ago a colleague in ministry urged that I compile for publication some of the worship resources I had created for the congregation we had served together. He said further that such a collection of resources should also include commentaries on their use liturgically. I chose a title based on a metaphor used by Paul in his conversation with the Corinthians: "Earthen Vessels." The publisher changed it to *Worship Vessels*[1] and designed a dust cover with graphics of shelves of round pottery water jars. Pottery jars are fragile things, easily broken, easily discarded. They are functional utensils, designed to hold their contents for storage toward an eventual eating or

---

1. F. Russell Mitman, *Worship Vessels: Resources for Renewal* (San Francisco: Harper & Row, 1987).

drinking or other consumption. The earthen vessels I shaped had disposable intentions for the worship of God in Christian assemblies. They were designed not as liturgical museum pieces to be bound in gilt-edged, leather-covered volumes like medieval illuminated psalters, but simply as earthen liturgical vessels to help to bring to expression conversations of ordinary earthly assemblies with their God. "We have this treasure (*thesauros* in Greek) in earthen vessels, to show that the transcendent power belongs to God and not to us." Since I was and am still an unrepentant lectionary preacher, those vessels for the doing of liturgy were shaped by the texts of the lectionaries that met particular assemblies week after week, year after year.

A decade later I still remembered my colleague's caveat that any worship vessel needed a commentary to aid the one who chooses a particular jar off the shelf—directions to be more pragmatic—as to its use in an assembly's doing liturgy. So, I began to explore what might be involved in the transposition of lectionary texts into liturgical expressions with Thomas Long's homiletical question as a guide: "How may the [liturgy], in a new setting, say and do what the text says and does in its setting?"[2] In other words, how may what the biblical text says and does in one genre say and do in a liturgical genre? I came to the conclusion that the same hermeneutic is involved in the shaping of liturgy in the shape of Scripture as in the creating of a sermon in the shape of Scripture. The Luke 4:26 hermeneutic outlined in the previous chapter again suggests the following: Today in this assembly gathered in this historic time and place, this Scripture, that is, a biblical text from a different time and place and therefore in a different genre, aims to be transposed for the assembly's doing liturgy (including the sermon) and to be fulfilled by the Holy Spirit in this assembly's hearing, speaking, singing, preaching, praying, dancing, gesturing, as an event of the Word of God. And the transcendent power for this transposition—if the Word of God is to happen in this liturgical doing at all—"belongs to God

2. Thomas G. Long, *Preaching and the Literary Forms of the Bible* (Philadelphia: Fortress, 1989), 33.

and not to us." The study I undertook intended to celebrate the marriage of homiletics and liturgics and to invite an acknowledgment of the hopefully not-so-radical notion that the entire worship service, not just the sermon, is a proclamatory event of the Word of God. The whole liturgy preaches. I suggested that this thesis be titled "From Lectionary to Liturgy: Worship in the Shape of Scripture," but again the publisher nixed the first part and went with the subtitle alone, *Worship in the Shape of Scripture*.[3]

Please pardon, dear reader, all these biographical excursions before reaching the present destination and the subject of this chapter, that "preaching *liturgically*" is different from "*liturgical* preaching." Again, to me, there is a fundamental difference between the intentions of *adjectives that describe some thing* and *adverbs that indicate how an action takes place*. "Liturgical preaching" describes a homiletical style in which the sermon is crafted in such a way that it relates to the other parts of the liturgy, particularly with the celebration of the eucharist.

Frequently those who speak and write about "liturgical preaching" assume officially prescribed texts for assemblies doing liturgy. Some seminary courses are offered on "preaching in a liturgical context." Again, given sets of texts and contexts are assumed into which a sermon or homily *is inserted*. "Preaching liturgically," I contend, is a way of an assembly's doing liturgy that allows the whole worship service to become a unified event of the Word of God.

In an article titled "The Function and Task of Liturgical Preaching," from an Orthodox perspective, Timothy Clark writes about what he calls the "liturgical sermon." He says, "The sermon's task is to preach the gospel to the assembly. Yet the sermon is not simply an evangelical oration which happens to be placed within the liturgy; *it is a fully liturgical action*."[4] Charles Rice a generation ago posed: "Can we find a place and a

---

3. F. Russell Mitman, *Worship in the Shape of Scripture* (Cleveland: Pilgrim, 2001, 2009).

4. Timothy Clark, "The Function and Task of Liturgical Preaching," *St. Vladimir's Theological Quarterly* 45, no. 1 (2001): 41; italics mine.

way to preach that faithfully resonate the Word of God seeking embodiment in bread, wine, water, human speech, and a community's interaction? Can we find a way of preaching that helps make all these factors and experiences an inseparable whole?"[5]

Daniel Stevick, who for years guided the course of liturgical renewal, wrote at the beginning of his *The Crafting of Liturgy*:

> The parts [of a liturgical event] should contribute to a convincing, satisfying whole. But there is a great deal that can go wrong. Elements can compete with or subvert one another. The strength of the spoken texts can be weakened by hymns that are too subjective, if they are not mawkishly sentimental. Strong, colorful ingredients can follow one another so closely that none of them shows up to advantage. Runaway virtuosity can heighten some nonessential action, while important acts are allowed to pass unnoticed. Or the liturgical event can be experienced as a series of parts that follow one another without shape, consecutiveness or flow. If the parts of an act of worship are to contribute to one another and if together they are to fashion a whole, there is need for care, for criteria, for thought, discrimination, and priorities. Shaping good liturgy is a craft. Rather than being a science, it is an art, calling for taste, judgement and design.[6]

As one who approached liturgy from an Anglican perspective, Stevick assumed a given liturgical framework for his recommendations. "Preparing worship," he continued, "in a church with an authorized liturgical text and preparing in a church without such a text are markedly different tasks. To adapt something that Robert Frost said about poetic meter and free verse: One is like playing tennis with a net and a marked court; the other is like playing tennis on an open field."[7]

5. Charles L. Rice, *The Embodied Word: Preaching as Art and Liturgy* (Minneapolis: Fortress, 1991), 18.

6. Daniel B. Stevick, *The Crafting of Liturgy* (New York: Church Hymnal Corporation, 1990), 5.

7. Stevick, *The Crafting of Liturgy*, 5.

What about those worship leaders serving on "open fields"? What approaches are appropriate and necessary for worship leaders who more and more find themselves liturgically on "unmarked courts" and "without nets"? My contention is that Stevick's goal to create a convincing, satisfying whole liturgically and homiletically is possible *also* in those churches *without* authorized liturgical texts printed in prayer books or hymnals that are in the hands of each worshiper weekly. It is indeed, in Stevick's words, "a markedly different task" for leaders to prepare worship for congregations not accustomed to doing liturgy from an authorized text even though the denominational parent-bodies may have prepared such texts. Generally, the liturgies prepared by denominational commissions and sometimes authorized by wider-church bodies appear in separate handbooks that are designed primarily for use by pastors and worship leaders. Some services also may be bound within hymnals for congregational use. Moreover, more recently published hymnals and worship books include multiple settings, some designed for specific seasons and Sundays in the church year. So, worship leaders on "unmarked courts" as well as those with liturgical "safety nets" in hymnals and worship books have the awesome responsibility of choosing or creating worship expressions from a plethora of resources in the weekly task of crafting a liturgical and homiletical whole that aims at enabling a worshiping assembly to be immersed in the splendor of God.

The issue facing worship leaders hinges on texts. In some ecclesial traditions worship is shaped by the givenness of liturgical texts, and the work of liturgiologists and even synods and councils of the church centers on authenticating and authorizing the texts, that is, the *words* of worship, and even translating those texts into different vernaculars. In those traditions in which there are no authorized liturgical texts or suggested or model liturgies or directories of worship, the crafting of what will happen in worship is left to the discretion of the congregation and/or the presider and preacher. These are the "open fields" of which Stevick spoke. "Liturgical preaching" in the former means, essentially, the insertion of a sermon into the given and sometimes unchangeable liturgical texts. In the no-text traditions, frequently "liturgical" is a negative description of what that particular worshiping assembly *is not*, and it is the preacher's sermon that decides whatever texts of prayers, hymns, and Scripture are chosen.

The argument between "texts" or "no texts" really does not help ecumenical conversations related to worship. Rather, studies have revealed an ecumenical convergence in the past half-century not because of the *words* of the texts themselves, but because of *what lies behind* the texts or even the no-texts. This is the common ordered sequence of acts identified as the *ordo* that gives shape to the worship event. In some traditions this sequence of acts is referred to as an "order of worship." The *ordo* is the common structure, the framework that has supported and shaped the worship life of churches historically and ecumenically.

I have had the privilege of working with an ecumenical group of liturgical scholars, pastors, and interested laypersons dedicated to liturgical renewal in the church. The group originated as a forum for dialogue between Episcopalians and Lutherans. Eventually the composition of the study group was widened to include ordained, religious, and lay Roman Catholics as well as priests in Orthodox churches and pastors and scholars in various branches of the Reformed community. In an ongoing discussion of what unites the common work of the Philadelphia Liturgical Institute, we began to focus on the unifying role of the *ordo*. I remember distinctly the day a Roman Catholic layperson who is a gifted architect held up a document he had retrieved from the Internet. It was titled "The Ordo: Center of Liturgical Reform," which was presented by Presbyterian liturgical scholar, Arlo Duba, to the organizing meeting of the Association for Reformed and Liturgical Worship in Seattle in 2005. All at once we had found a shared point of reference for subsequent ecumenical liturgical discussions and work.

The *ordo*, indeed, is the common ground that unites all the individual worship words and actions into a unified whole. And a sermon or homily within the *ordo* is not an insertion but an integral act of what aims at being a total event of the Word of God. Preaching liturgically, I maintain, is not a *style* of sermonizing but an approach to worship that allows the whole action of the assembly to become a unified act of proclamation.

The counsel of a gifted director of music in one of the congregations I served still echoes in my mind: "Russ, if you think you have everybody together with you at every point throughout the service, you are deceiving yourself!" My research and experience across the years have proven her counsel wise and true. Individuals in any assembly come to each worship event with their own life-texts. Each brings his or her hurts and hopes in the expectation that in Word and Sacrament God will touch those hurts and hopes with divine grace. Yet, doing liturgy is not an individual devotion between "me and my God." Doing liturgy is *corporate* work. So, how in a collection of individual hurts and hopes can there be a *corporate* experience of the divine presence?

I learned from the architectural philosophy and practice of Frank Lloyd Wright and others in the Arts and Crafts Movement that each individual architectural motif, even as small as a table lamp or candle holder, was designed to be a part of an organic whole. I learned, too, from French Impressionists, particularly those experimenting in creating paintings of dots of pure color (pointillism), that the individual dots together in the eye and mind of the beholder create a unified image. This very page I am writing in my computerized word processor is a collection of infinitesimal electronic dots called "pixels" that together form alphabetical letters and words. So, I coined the phrase "organic liturgy" in which each separate expression, even an individual word or musical or graphic motif, is meant to be part of an organic whole. And since one worshiper may be drawn into the event through one expression and another worshiper through another expression, the *corporate* doing of liturgy is possible.

Unfortunately, sometimes some traditions have interpreted their freedom from adherence to prescribed liturgical texts as a license for an anything-goes approach to worship. Yet, the goal of a liturgy that aims at a unified event is not to create a monolithic service revolving around some central theme. Thematic services based on holiday celebrations or on topics that are of the worship leader's preference or of the assembly's liking often are manipulative and designed to have the worshipers experience what the leader wants them to experience. In *organic* liturgy all the individual acts, including the sermon, *grow out* of an engagement with the biblical texts and interact with each other homiletically and liturgically to enable the *leitourgia*, literally the "work," of the assembly to take place.

The interconnectedness associated with an organic approach to homiletics and liturgics is fundamentally a reflection of the very nature of the church itself, in New Testament images, as the *body* of Christ with Christ at the center and all the members working in harmony. The whole of worship is a total event of integrally related and mutually dependent acts through which the Word of God seeks embodiment in the community of faith.

My research and consulting with congregations testify that one worshiper may experience the presence of God through a particular hymn, another through a Scripture reading, another through a prayer, and, even, another through the sermon. We preachers sometimes have the inflated notion that everything in worship centers on the sermon! Charles Rice characterized sermon-centered worship in the image of "a kind of homiletical ocean liner preceded by a few liturgical tugboats!"[8] The experience of the pew-sitters is very different! The intention of crafting organic liturgy is to attempt to bring all the dots together into a unified homiletical and liturgical whole that will, even in the distortions of human words, sounds, images, and actions, aim to draw the whole assembly holistically into an event of the Word of God. Liturgics and homiletics are not separate yet related disciplines as "liturgical preaching" or "preaching in a liturgical context" imply, but *integrated* arts organically wedded in a common praxis aimed at enabling the entire worship

---

8. Rice, *The Embodied Word*, 31.

service to become a preaching event in which *all assembled* in a variety of common expressions and roles proclaim the one Word of God, Jesus Christ. In Paul's epistle to the Corinthian church he writes, *kēryssomen Christon . . .* (we preach Christ . . .). The verb that gets translated as "preach" or "proclaim" is in the first person *plural: "we* preach." The grammatical person and tense of the Greek verb that Paul—or his scribe—used can be the subject of a study of Paul's literary style or inquiry into grammatical constructions. Yet, "we preach" invites us theologically to get beyond the grammar and to approach being immersed *corporately* into the very mystery of what happens in Word and Sacrament. It is not insignificant that the root of "corporately" in Latin is *corpus,* "body," and in the Latin version of Paul's letters, "body of Christ" is *corpus Christi.*

I can remember approaching Sunday's sermon with a #2 pencil and a yellow legal pad with blue lines. My desk was in front of a window, and I recall staring out the window and at the blank page wondering what in the world I would have to say. The trouble was that I was still approaching the homiletical task as something distinct from liturgical crafting. Eventually, with the help of electronic word processing, I learned to integrate the two. The "windows" were no longer transparent panes of glass through which I looked out into the wild blue yonder, but electronic pages in electronic files that I open simultaneously and work interchangeably between one "window" that contains the lectionary texts appointed for a forthcoming Sunday, another "window" that gets labeled with the name of that Sunday in the church year plus the date in which the liturgy will be shaped, and a third "window" that will include a focus text or texts for the sermon.

I learned from Paul Scott Wilson that the homiletical/liturgical work begins with spending at least twenty minutes with the texts, allowing them prayerfully and meditatively to penetrate the homiletical and liturgical imagination.[9] I have

9. Paul Scott Wilson, *Imagination of the Heart: New Understandings in Preaching* (Nashville: Abingdon, 1988).

encountered the same texts in the same three-year lectionary cycle for decades. Yet, each time something new jumps out of the text. I appreciate the times that I can spend with groups in the congregation being engaged together by the texts. New images emerge corporately that stimulate my work in the days beyond the initial engagement. Words, hymns, and prayer fragments begin to emerge in these encounters that get inserted into the "liturgy" window and/or the "sermon" window.

Then, the crafting of the liturgy and sermon for the forthcoming Sunday begins—simultaneously. Yes, crafting the liturgy for the assembly's worship-work and the sermon that will be an integral part of the assembly's worship is a *common* task that, hopefully, results in a unified liturgical/homiletical experience of the Word of God arising organically from and shaped by the Scriptures. I constantly find myself in the midst of the homiletical/liturgical crafting already experiencing as a foretaste what will occur in the forthcoming worship event with the assembly. Preparing for worship, for me, is already participating in worship. Perhaps that is a reminder that each worship event is a proleptic participation in the kingdom of God that is already but not yet. I will elaborate on this in subsequent chapters.

The shaping does not begin with a blank page. Rather, the "window" of the assembly's corporate activity has been open for years. It's called the *ordo*, that is, the ordered sequence of actions that have shaped Christian worship historically and ecumenically and that arise from the Scriptures themselves:

> *Gathering* (including penitential acts that sometimes constitute a separate action)
> *Word* (Scripture, sermon, and prayers)
> *Eucharist* (holy communion, Lord's Supper)
> *Sending*

This ordered sequence is not some arbitrary construction of liturgical scholars or ecclesial bodies, or even just a product of historical practice. Gordon Lathrop in the first of his liturgical trilogy, *Holy Things: A Liturgical Theology*, begins with a chapter titled "The Biblical Pattern of Liturgy."[10] "Begin with the Bible," he says in the first sentence. "To discern the form and articulate the crucial meaning of the Christian assembly we may look especially there. The Bible marks and largely determines Christian corporate worship. It is fair to say that the liturgies of the diverse churches all have a biblical character."[11] And he continues in the second chapter, which he titled "Basic Patterns in the *Ordo* of Christian Worship": "Meaning occurs through structure by one thing set next to another. The scheduling of the *ordo*, the setting of one liturgical thing next to another in the shape of the liturgy, evokes and replicates the deep structure of biblical language."[12] It was he who inspired me and gave "license" to me in the formation of *Worship in the Shape of Scripture*.

Some of the individual expressions in the *ordo* in some churches do not change from week to week, season to season. In the congregation I presently am serving, certain expressions such as the Kyrie, the Peace, Apostles' Creed, and Lord's Prayer do not change, or rarely change, so that they can be memorized and enable people with limited sight and reading skills to participate in the corporate action. I have begun to hear small voices saying, "Lord, have mercy on us" and singing, "Gloria, Gloria in excelsis Deo!" One mother told me recently that her four-year-old son has "church" at home and speaks the words he has memorized through weekly participation in the assembly's liturgy—and in the "order" of those expressions! I learned in confirmation formation with groups of teenagers that, when I asked "What happens in worship," they could tell me the *sequence* of acts within the order of worship. They knew the *ordo* by doing the *ordo*. That is one reason children need to participate regularly—and not just occasionally—in worship. The *ordo* is not simply words and actions printed in prayer books or in

10. Gordon W. Lathrop, *Holy Things: A Liturgical Theology* (Minneapolis: Augsburg Fortress, 1993).
11. Lathrop, *Holy Things*, 15.
12. Lathrop, *Holy Things*, 33.

weekly pamphlets or on projection screens or video monitors. It is stored in the assembly's corporate and individual memory.

The *ordo* is stored as a template in my "liturgy" window, and in shaping the corporate expressions from week to week some stay there from perhaps the former week or from the same Sunday in the lectionary cycle or from another Sunday in the church year. The *ordo* provides the structure or framework that brings cohesion to the individual expressions and, in the corporate memory of the worshiping community, provides continuity from week to week, season to season. The *ordo* is a corporate lived experience *that in its totality* attempts to fulfill Paul's "We preach Christ." Each Sunday in the church I serve, the five words of the *ordo* are printed as headings and thus reminders of the liturgical action in which the assembly is engaged with the Word of God: "Gathering, Penitence, Word, Eucharist, Sending."

And, in most traditions, that ordered corporate experience of the Word of God includes something called a sermon or homily. The third "window" that is opened in each week's crafting of the worship event is the file called "sermon." Eventually the words and thoughts that have been entered into this file as the liturgy has been taking shape—eventually these shape themselves into what will emerge as the sermon or homily. The sermon, I have found, really writes itself. And I unashamedly "write" each sermon word for word because each word is a tiny part of a much larger collage. And if all of these individual pieces—including everything that will be spoken, sung, or enacted by the assembly—aim at being an event of the Word of God, I sometimes labor over each word not to make sure it is the "right word," but a word that when spoken and heard in the totality of the worship event may be used by the Holy Spirit to communicate the Word of God. Preaching Christ is an awesome art.

3

Preaching **Sacramentally**

Has not God made foolish the wisdom of the world? For since, in the wisdom of God, the world did not know God through wisdom, God decided, through the foolishness of our proclamation, to save those who believe.

—1 Corinthians 1:20–21

Now among those who went up to worship at the festival were some Greeks. They came to Philip, who was from Bethsaida in Galilee, and said to him, "Sir, we wish to see Jesus."

—John 12:20–21

It is interesting how the words of Paul to the church at Corinth have been translated into English in the last four hundred years. The King James Version (1611) translated the noun *kērygma* as "preaching," and the verb *kēryssō* as "preach." By 1946 the Revised Standard Version translated these respectively as "what we preach" and "preach." By the release of the New Revised Standard Version in 1989, the noun became "proclamation," and the verb "we proclaim." By 2011 "preaching" and "preach" return in the Common English Bible. It is more than an exercise in linguistics to see how translators have grappled with a Greek noun and verb that are almost untranslatable in modern understandings of English words that have attracted all sorts of positive and negative images. Most of those images are barnacles left over from English vessels that have sailed through the waters from post-Reformation orthodoxy through Enlightenment reasonings and even fundamentalist biblical literalisms.

Paul lifts *kērygma* and *kēryssō* above the seekings of philosophists and entices the Christian community at Corinth to experience through preaching/proclamation the power of Christ to bring about a new life in a new community. As such, preaching/proclamation is a transformative means of grace. Paul goes on to say to the Corinthians, "[God] is the source of your life in Christ Jesus, who became for us wisdom from God, and righteousness and sanctification and redemption" (1 Cor. 1:30). So "preaching Christ" is not simply a dissertation *about* Christ, but a proclamation of the Word that *is* Christ. Christ is *present*-ed in the preaching/proclamation and is present in the community through not only the *homilia* of the preacher but through the words and actions, the *leitourgia*, of the whole assembly. When, in Paul's saying, "We preach Christ," we preach/proclaim a Christ who in the very act of that preaching/proclamation is as sacramentally present as a means of grace as Christ is present in the sacraments of baptism and eucharist. The entire preaching event in an assembly's encounter with the Word of God, in this sense, is nothing less than sacramental. And the *action* of engaging and participating in a conversation with the Word of God, preaching Christ, is preaching sacramentally: presenting Christ who promises to be present *in the presenting*.

Martha Moore-Keish, in her book on Reformed eucharistic theology, provides an insightful commentary on a basic shift in eucharistic emphasis that occurred during the Reformation of the sixteenth century. She writes, "The primary question about a ritual shifted from 'What does it *do*?' to 'What does it *mean*?'"[1] She illustrates with a reference to the Marburg Colloquy of 1529 during which Martin Luther and Ulrich Zwingli

---

1. Martha Moore-Keish, *Do This in Remembrance of Me: A Ritual Approach to Reformed Eucharistic Theology* (Grand Rapids: Eerdmans, 2008), 15–16.

were invited by Prince Philip of Hesse to his castle in the hopes of reconciling differences between the two of them. At the beginning of discussions Luther reportedly wrote on the table in front of him, "*Hoc est corpus meum*," interpreting the "*est*" literally: "This *is* my body" in some mysterious way we cannot comprehend.[2] In the eucharist, in Luther's view, Christ is present "in, with, and under" the elements of bread and wine. Note that the emphasis is on the action, the *doing*. Luther was simply repeating what the church had maintained for centuries when liturgical theologians spoke of "doing" the liturgy.

Zwingli, on the other hand, maintained—and here is the shift—the "*is*" means "signifies"; it points to something beyond itself. Luther, Moore-Keish continues, "used the language of 'essence.' . . . 'Let us not try to inquire how Christ's body is in the Lord's Supper. . . . He is in the sacrament (but) not as in a place.' The efficacy of the sacrament depends on God's words, not on human faith, according to Luther. Thus his emphasis was on the objectivity of the gift in the Supper."[3] "Zwingli's emphasis was on the faith of the believers which was publicly professed at communion. . . . The body of Christ is in the Supper *representatively*."[4] A theological battle with huge ecclesial and political consequences was on.

Moore-Keish goes on to point out that the second-generation reformer, John Calvin, sought to mediate between Lutheran and Zwinglian views on the eucharist. "Early in his section on the Lord's Supper in the *Institutes*, [Calvin] lists two 'faults' to guard against: 'too little regard for signs, thus divorcing them from their mysteries, and too much regard for signs, thus obscuring the mysteries themselves.'" She continues, "The first fault is that of Zwingli, the second, that of Luther. Calvin always sought to balance respect for the 'signs,' the embodied reality of the eucharistic event, and respect for the 'mysteries,' that is,

---

2. Moore-Keish, *Do This in Remembrance of Me*, 17.
3. Moore-Keish, *Do This in Remembrance of Me*, 18–19.
4. Moore-Keish, *Do This in Remembrance of Me*, 19.

the living Christ who cannot be contained in the event."[5] Calvin emphasized the "spiritual real presence" of Christ in the eucharist and insisted on weekly communion but was overruled on the latter by Genevan civil and religious authorities.

In the nineteenth century a significant movement to rediscover Calvin's eucharistic theology began in the Seminary of the Reformed Church in the USA in Mercersburg, Pennsylvania. John Williamson Nevin in 1846 wrote a lengthy defense of Calvin's perspective on the "real" presence in a book called *The Mystical Presence*, with the subtitle *A Vindication of the Reformed or Calvinistic Doctrine of the Holy Eucharist*.[6] Other significant attempts to "vindicate" Calvin's sacramental theology against those who identify "Reformed" with predominantly Zwinglian understandings continue in many settings today.

The two emphases on the faith of the believer and the objective means of grace are united as early as 1563 in the Heidelberg Catechism. This statement of faith in catechizing format was commissioned by Emperor Frederick III of the Palatinate in an attempt to bring together Lutheran and Reformed constituencies in this politically powerful region in southwest Germany. It was penned largely by Zacharias Ursinus, a student of another great mediator, Philip Melanchthon. Note how "meaning" and "doing" are carefully joined in Question 76: "What does it mean to eat the crucified body and drink the shed blood of Christ?" The answer:

> It is not only to embrace with a trusting heart all the sufferings and death of Christ, and by so doing receive the forgiveness of sins and eternal life, but also to be united more and more to his sacred body through the Holy Spirit who dwells both in Christ and in us, so that, although he is in heaven and we are on earth, we nevertheless are flesh of his flesh

5. Moore-Keish, *Do This in Remembrance of Me*, 19–20.

6. John W. Nevin, *The Mystical Presence: A Vindication of the Reformed or Calvinistic Doctrine of the Holy Eucharist* (Philadelphia: J. B. Lippincott & Co., 1846).

and bone of his bone, and live and are governed forever by one Spirit, just as the members of our bodies are governed by one soul.[7]

In a previous question: "Then, since faith alone makes us share in Christ and all his blessings, where does such faith come from?" The answer: "The Holy Spirit awakens it in our hearts by the preaching of the holy gospel, and confirms it by the use of the holy sacraments."[8] Note the unity of "Word" and "Sacrament," an understanding shared by both Lutheran and Reformed theologians of the Reformation. Note also the element of objective action of divine grace through the Holy Spirit who "awakens" faith and "confirms" faith "by the use of," in other words, by *doing* the sacramental actions. And, thirdly, note that "sacraments" are plural, and in Question 68 the sacraments are numbered as two: "baptism" and the "Lord's Supper"—even though questions lingered in 1563 and still do around what is sacramental. And can sacraments really be numbered? What is clear is that within less than fifty years after the beginning of the Reformation in Wittenberg in 1517 we find the affirmation that there is one Word, Jesus Christ, who is really present in one unified liturgical event of the Word of God through preaching and the sacraments.

The dichotomy between "What does it mean?" and "What does it do?" that Moore-Keish identified in relation to the eucharist also set in with respect to preaching. The Reformers' need to teach the meaning of what happens in worship and to communicate the meaning of biblical texts led in later generations to an excessive didacticism in preaching. Sermons became long expositions of biblical texts, in some traditions by means of a *lectio continuo* of reading and preaching through a whole book of the Bible, chapter after chapter, verse after verse. During the days of Protestant orthodoxy the need for defining

7. *The Heidelberg Catechism: A New Translation for the 21st Century*, trans. Lee C. Barrett (Cleveland: Pilgrim, 2007), 91.
8. *The Heidelberg Catechism*, 82.

the new understandings of the faith resulted in lengthy discourses on doctrine. Homiletics, which became fertile ground for the implanting of an eighteenth-century Enlightenment focus on the role of human reason, turned sermons into rational arguments designed to communicate biblical and doctrinal truths. Pews were introduced so assemblies could sit to hear the preacher, and the preachers' skills centered on the art of persuasion. In eighteenth-century American churches, deacons with long poles to which feathers were attached awakened the dozing from sermonic slumber.

Yet, the Cranach altarpiece in the Stadtkirche in Wittenberg, to which I referred in chapter 1, depicts a very different homiletical theology. First of all, the assembly was not asleep! Second, it was intergenerational; kids were not sent off to a separate Sunday school during worship. And, most importantly, the primary purpose of preaching as this painting depicts is not to impart some doctrinal *meaning* of Christ but, on the basis of a biblical text, to preach Christ, to *present* a crucified and risen Christ who *is* present through the Holy Spirit in the midst of the worshiping assembly.

The painting is the base of a three-paneled triptych portraying baptism, holy communion, and absolution. The juxtaposition of the panels raises the question: Does that third panel hint at a third "sacrament"? And does the preaching-Christ base of the triptych intend to put preaching in the same sacramental picture? Luther did speak of preaching along with baptism and eucharist as signs of the true church. So did Calvin, and so have many of the faithful since then. Cranach did not depict Luther pointing to the sacraments. Rather, he points to the one Christ, who at the base of the triptych is present in the assembly and therefore is present in the sacramental acts that the assembly *does*. The portrayal of the sacraments does not focus on the elements of the sacraments or even the furniture of worship but on the *actions* of the sacramental acts—including what the preaching does—to *present* (verb) Christ. And the whole altarpiece—including its placement behind the altar in the Stadtkirche—is designed to portray an organic whole. The whole triptych itself preaches sacramentally. It is dated 1547, and, by the way, the vesture of the assemblies and the presiders and preachers is "contemporary," in the literal meaning of the word "con-temporary": "with the times"—of the sixteenth century! The German theologian and pastor Dietrich Bonhoeffer, who was martyred by the Nazis at the end of World War II for his opposition to Hitler, used a wonderful homiletical metaphor in his lectures on preaching at the Confessing Church seminary in Finkenwalde. He wrote: "The proclaimed word is the incarnate Christ himself. As little as the incarnation is the outward shape of God, just so little does the proclaimed word present the outward form of a reality; rather, it is the thing itself. The preached Christ is both the Historical One and the Present One. . . . Therefore the proclaimed word is not a medium of expression for something else, something which lies behind it, but rather it is the Christ himself walking through his congregation as the Word."[9] Samuel Giere comments, "In short, Bonhoeffer speaks of the sermon as the *sacramentum verbi*—'the sacrament of the word.' The Word does what it is, and is what it does."[10] Preaching sacramentally, opening the door in the whole liturgical event for Christ to walk through the congregation I am serving each Sunday, is truly an awesome privilege and responsibility. Preaching sacramentally is an approach to both homiletics and liturgics that takes us beyond entertainment to engagement, beyond "audience" to assembly, beyond "How many are in attendance?" to "Who is gathered?" By the way, in Cranach's painting of the assembly in the Stadtkirche I can count only about eighteen people gathered, one of whom supposedly is Luther's wife and two of whom are Luther's kids! Preaching sacramentally is accompanying liturgically Christ on his weekly walk through the assembly of souls searching to touch the hem of his garment, and Christ takes the walk even

9. Dietrich Bonhoeffer, *Worldly Preaching: Lectures on Homiletics*, ed. and trans. Clyde E. Fant (New York: Thomas Nelson, 1975), 126.
10. Samuel Giere, "Preaching as Sacrament of the Word," blog post, Monday, January 5, 2009.

if there are but two or three gathered. And it takes the same homiletical and liturgical integrity on the part of preachers and presiders to prepare for Christ's weekly walk regardless of whether two or two thousand show up!

Preaching sacramentally is the very act of participating in the enacting of a mystery. Bonhoeffer put it this way: "When a preacher opens [the] Bible and interprets the word of God, a mystery takes place, a miracle: the grace of God, who comes down from heaven into our midst and speaks to us, knocks on our door, asks questions, warns us, puts pressure on us, alarms us, threatens us, and makes us joyful again and free and sure. When the Holy Scriptures are brought to life in a church, the Holy Spirit comes down from the eternal throne, into our hearts."[11] John Burgess speaks of "Scripture as Sacramental Word." "What makes Scripture *Scripture*," he says, "is its capacity to mediate an encounter with the transcendent."[12] Burgess continues, "As a sacramental word, Scripture is not only a witness, however unique or authoritative, to the revelation that has taken place in Christ; rather, Scripture as *Scripture* also sets forth the living Christ. It draws us into the possibility of relationship between the divine and the human."[13]

Nelle Morton taught me many years ago the importance of the visual symbol of the Bible being opened physically at the beginning of worship. I also learned from the Scottish liturgical tradition the role of the *beadle*, a lay leader in the church, who carries the Bible to the pulpit and opens it, as if to say, "Here, preacher, is the Word," and in the words of the Greeks who said to Philip according to John 12:21 and which are inscribed on many Scottish pulpits visible only to the preacher, "We wish to see Jesus." Enabling the assembly to see Jesus multivalently is the intention of preaching sacramentally. And through the prayer

11. Bonhoeffer, *Creation and Fall*, Dietrich Bonhoeffer Works, vol. 3, ed. Geffrey B. Kelly, trans. Daniel W. Bloesch and James H. Burtness (Minneapolis: Fortress, 2005), 323.

12. John P. Burgess, *Why Scripture Matters: Reading the Bible in a Time of Church Conflict* (Louisville: Westminster John Knox, 1998), 41.

13. Burgess, *Why Scripture Matters*, 41.

of illumination that precedes the reading of Scripture and the preaching, on behalf of both assembly, lectors, and preacher(s), in Colossians 4:3, the common prayer is "that God will open to us a door for the word, that we may declare the mystery of Christ."

The work of homileticians and liturgiologists in the latter half of the twentieth century led to the reunification of the events of preaching and eucharist into one liturgical action. "Word and Sacrament" or "Word and Table" became the headings of many mainline Protestant denominations' liturgies. The attempt was made again to affirm that eucharist is normative for every Lord's Day. The earlier practice of providing one liturgy that includes holy communion and one without communion gradually was eliminated. In some instances variant endings were provided if eucharist was not celebrated. The *ordos* in the liturgies of most mainline churches in the last half-century or so years affirm the unity of acts of preaching and celebrating the sacrament.

Yet, the question remains regarding the organic *unity* of the Word preached and enacted in the sacraments. Some recent Roman Catholic and Orthodox liturgical theologians are hinting at more holistic approaches to homiletics and liturgics. The United States Conference of Catholic Bishops published in 2012 a document, *Preaching the Mystery of Faith: The Sunday Homily*. "The fundamental pattern of preaching in the Emmaus narrative illustrates the essential connection between Scripture, the homily, and the Eucharist; for it was in the 'breaking of the bread' that the disciples ultimately recognized their Risen Lord, and it was then they realized that their hearts were burning within them 'while he spoke to us on the way and opened the Scriptures to us' (Lk 24:32)."[14] Father Jeremy Driscoll elaborates on the bishops' statement: "That is to say, there is a sense in which the experience of Eucharist casts its force backwards to the Liturgy of the Word, revealing only now, in Eucharist, how much was already present in the Scriptures. Wanting to secure this wonderful connection, the bishops offer a very explicit di-

---

14. *Preaching the Mystery of Faith: The Sunday Homily*, United States Conference of Catholic Bishops, Washington, DC, 2012.

rective and in so doing are certainly wanting to push preaching in a new direction by this document."[15]

Fr. Driscoll's explication of the bishops' document seems to suggest that it was only the experience of the breaking of the bread, that is, the eucharist, that gave sacramental legitimacy to the opening of the Scriptures: "The experience of the Eucharist casts its force backwards to the Liturgy of the Word." His "backwards" hermeneutic seems to intimate that without eucharist there would be no sacramental action in the opening of the Scriptures, that is, there would be no real presence of Christ in the preaching. One could ask the reverse question: "Would the action of breaking the bread be sufficient itself without the preaching of the Word?" In some circles that was and still is affirmed and is the practice.

There is an axiom in some circles that sacramental preaching is about linking words and images in the sermon with actions in the meal. From a literary and rhetorical perspective such linkages are appropriate. Yet, this perspective still assumes two separate liturgical actions joined by verbal mechanics, and begs the question: "Is the Lord fully present in both preached Word and broken bread in one sacrament of the mystery of Jesus Christ proclaimed *and* enacted?"

Orthodox theologian Alexander Schmemann forty years ago addressed the problem of dividing the Orthodox Divine Liturgy into two separate elements. He wrote: "In the Orthodox perspective the liturgy of the Word is as sacramental as the sacrament is 'evangelical.' The sacrament is a manifestation of the Word. And unless the false dichotomy between Word and Sacrament is overcome, the true meaning of both Word and Sacrament, and especially the true meaning of Christian 'sacramentalism,' cannot be grasped in all their wonderful implications."[16]

15. Jeremy Driscoll, OSB, "Catechesis and Doctrine in Liturgical Preaching," 2013 USCCB Conference on "Preaching the Mystery of Faith," October 1, 2013, 6.

16. Alexander Schmemann, *For the Life of the World* (Crestwood, NY: St. Vladimir's Seminary Press, 1973), 33.

Preaching sacramentally, then, to me is approaching and practicing homiletics and liturgics with the intention of opening the assembly to the mystery of God in *all* the individual elements of a unified enactment of the one Word of God. In such an approach the question of what constitutes a sacrament is the opening to a mystery undefined and the means of grace innumerable. Preaching sacramentally is the bonding of homiletics and liturgics in a unified approach to the encounter of the assembly with one Word God who promises to be present in manifold and mysterious ways.

Any discussion of Word and Sacrament cannot continue without touching on baptism. Preaching sacramentally is preaching baptismally—yes, "baptismally" is an adverb my word processor accepts! Preaching sacramentally sees baptism as the sacramental context for the event of the Word of God. In some times and settings proclamation leads to a baptism that is yet to happen. Yet always, baptism is the defining of an assembly's doings liturgically and homiletically. The assembly is gathered each Lord's Day with the sign of baptism in the name of the Trinity. The assembly is sent into the world each Lord's Day with the sign of baptism and the blessing of the triune God. Worship begins at the font, and worship sends at the font. And the whole of worship—Word and Sacrament—is enacted in an immersion in baptism's sacramental waters.

Baptism is the one-time, initiating sacrament. Baptism is something that happens to each individual. Yet baptism is also the universal act that defines the church and unites all the baptized—and even the unbaptized. A generous gift to the universal church is the document *Invitation to Christ: A Guide to Sacramental Practices*[17] first created by the Office of Worship of the Presbyterian Church USA and subsequently published in an ecumenical edition by the Association for Reformed and Liturgical Worship. What makes this document helpful is that sacramental practice leads to pedagogy. That is, assemblies en-

17. Lousiville: Presbyterian Church (USA), a Corporation, on behalf of the Office of Theology and Worship, 2006.

gaging in the five sacramental practices are led into deeper meanings of baptism and eucharist. Three of the five suggested practices are particularly related to baptism: "1. Set the font in full view of the congregation. 2. Open the font and fill it with water on every Lord's Day. . . . 4. Lead appropriate parts of weekly worship from the font and from the table." In most older and smaller congregations baptisms rarely occur, and fonts frequently are pushed to side aisles or even relegated to closets. The sacramental practices outlined in *Invitation to Christ* invite assemblies into the sacraments that define them. I have discovered that children as well as older adults appreciate the opportunity to engage in the nonverbal aspects of these practices: seeing and hearing the water splash into the font, touching the water with their fingers, placing the water and the sign of the cross on their foreheads or as a blessing on others. The practices proclaim, and assemblies begin to discover, the deeper, mystical meanings that lie beyond words. Further, these baptismal practices unite the whole age spectrum of the assembly in a common experience. One couple on the occasion of their fiftieth wedding anniversary, for the first time in their lives, came to the font, dipped their fingers in the water, and placed the sign of blessing on each other's foreheads. That truly was a moment, nonverbally, in which *they* were the preachers preaching sacramentally to all who had eyes to see.

4

Preaching Evangelically

> For Christ did not send me to baptize but to proclaim the gospel, and not with eloquent wisdom, so that the cross of Christ might not be emptied of its power.
>
> —1 Corinthians 1:17

In 1817, on the occasion of the 300th anniversary of Luther's supposed posting of his theses for debate that had led to the Reformation of the sixteenth century, Emperor Frederick William III, with the support of theologian and pastor Friedrich Schleiermacher, proposed and royally effected a union of Reformed and Lutheran churches within the Prussian territories. This United Church of the Prussian Union brought most Protestant churches under the umbrella of the Evangelical Church of the Union (*Evangelische Kirche der Union*), which eventuated in the Union of Evangelical Churches. So, "*evangelisch*" as an adjective in German understandings means "Protestant." And to a lesser or greater degree, depending on the territory, *evangelisch* refers to a *united* Protestant church. People identify themselves as *evangelisch* or, on the other side of the sixteenth-century divide, as *katholisch*. In German there is no noun-form of a person identified by the adjective *evangelisch*, yet there are nouns for the Roman Catholic: *Katholik* if the person is male, *Katholikin* if female!

One of the great tragedies in American church life has been the hostage-taking of the word "evangelical" by religious fundamentalism. In American ecclesiology "evangelical" has morphed into both an adjective and a noun. The adjective, rather than a uniting word as in German churches, has become divisive. "Evangelical" as an adjective has become attached to a certain brand of American Protestantism that had its origins in Puritan pietism and the American "Great Awakening" of the eighteenth century. Its emphasis on mission and evangelism shaped America in the nineteenth century and led to the great missionary enterprises that spread the movement's message throughout the third world. It gave birth to and fostered religious and ideological fundamentalism in the twentieth century and to ideas of biblical inerrancy and anti-science "isms" that continue to infect public discourse and certain public school curricula. It also shaped American society and cultural norms, and by the latter half of the twentieth century became allied with certain political personalities and ideological agendas. Hence "evangelical" has become a brand by which some people positively identify themselves religiously, culturally, and politically.

On the other hand, "evangelical" is deemed by others as religiously sectarian, culturally exclusive, dedicated to "restoring" bygone values, and politically allied with rightwing ideologies. Hence, "evangelical" also has grown its noun-form: "evangelical" as a person, pronounced "*ee*vangelical." Both as an adjective and as a noun, "evangelical" has lost its original meaning and pronunciation in media and marketplace. Some would say that the word "evangelical" has been hijacked!

The root of "evangelical" is the Greek *euangelion*, generally translated into English as "gospel," "good news," from Old English *godspel* (translation of Late Latin *evangelium*), from *god* ("good") + *spell* ("tale"). *Euangelion* occurs forty-one times in the New Testament, depending on which Greek concordance is used, generally equally spread through the Pauline letters and the four Gospels with a few occurrences in the Pastoral Epistles and the book of Revelation. The verb form *euangelizō*, generally translated into English as "preach," occurs ninety-eight times in various verb constructions, active and passive, again depending on the concordance used. Unfortunately there is no good modern English translation for "gospel" *as a verb.* The person who "gospels" (my translation) is an *euangelistēs,* translated as "evangelist." yet it occurs in the New Testament only three times. Also, in the New Testament's Greek there is no adjectival or adverbial form. "Evangelical" as an adjective never occurs in the Bible. And "evangelically," although a grammatically correct adverb in English, is virtually nonexistent even among theological word-nerds!

A lot of print (the old-fashioned stuff) as well as electronic print on the Internet has been devoted to "evangelical preaching." Evangelical preachers found media first in radio and then in television in the twentieth century. Great empires were built by evangelical preachers, some stationed behind TV cameras, and others circuit-rider style in mass rallies in sports arenas. The goals of evangelical preaching generally were and are personal conversion and faith-formation, which may lead to baptism and, unfortunately, sometimes to rebaptism. Worship is essentially a long sermon sprinkled with snippets of Scripture, preceded by enthusiastic and emotional singing and appended with an "altar call" designed to lead to the sinner's repentance and conversion.

"Evangelistic" preaching has the same intention. It intends to be instrumental, that is, to lead to something in the hearer that will trigger the individual willfully to *do* something—generally to make a public affirmation of his or her faith in Christ, sometimes coupled with an individual confession of sins, and always with the intention morally and religiously to change one's life. The focus of evangelistic preaching is to convince and motivate the hearer to arrive at a faith-decision that is immediate and consciously definable.

Those who practice evangelistic preaching often are called or call themselves "evangelists." Charismatic appointment, either self-imposed or by prayer and laying on of hands by a bishop-type, is more important than and prior to any ecclesiastical endorsement or ordination. I am always amazed that the ranks of evangelists most often are restricted to those groups espousing an evangelical theology and ecclesiology.

Yet, St. Paul wrote to the Ephesians that the "gifts [Christ] gave were that some would be apostles, some prophets, some evangelists, some pastors and teachers, to equip the saints for the work of ministry, for building up the body of Christ" (Eph. 4:11–12), and Timothy is reminded to "do the work of an evangelist, carry out your ministry fully" (2 Tim. 4:5). The only other reference to an "evangelist" is a report in Acts where Paul and his companions went "into the house of Philip the evangelist" (Acts 21:8). In some ecclesiastical traditions today clergy are ordained as "pastor and teacher," yet these traditions are shy about "evangelist" and "prophet." And indeed the office of "apostle" was closed a long time ago pretty much except for some in the Latter Day Saints movement.

Then there is the verb form, "evangelize," which does not appear in the New Testament. Yet, throughout the Christian experience there have been many movements dedicated to "evangelize," that is, to convert to Christianity the heathens and unchurched, sometimes by physical coercion, by military conquest, by royal decree, or even by mind control. Although the Greek root *eu* ("good") + *angelizō* ("announce") is the purpose of preaching in the New Testament, the perversions throughout history have tainted "to evangelize" as an enterprise in which fewer and fewer want to engage.

Likewise, the noun form, "evangelism," although a noble cause by definition, has become synonymous in the popular mind with intrusive and sometimes obnoxious door-to-door conversion campaigns. "Evangelism" has become the "E-word" that, unfortunately, many churches and their preachers try to avoid, even though announcing the good news either by report or by command occurs in more than a hundred verses in the New Testament. To evangelize lies at the heart of the gospel; it *is* the gospel. On the other hand, when efforts to evangelize morph into programs to proselytize, what is intended to be "good news" ends up too often being bad news for the victims.

From a theological and biblical perspective, I would like to restore "gospel" as a verb: "to gospel." God is both subject and object of "to gospel." To preach evangelically, then, is "to gospel" (as an action) through the translucent lens of a scriptural text what God is doing *now*. To gospel (verb) is not restricted to what happens through the preacher's sermon. To gospel is the intention of an assembly gathered to *do* liturgy, and that corporate doing includes a sermon as one part of an integrated act of proclamation of the gospel. The whole worship event gospels. And gospeling continues during the week as the assembly individually encounters an increasingly frightened and despairing world.

This morning, as I am writing this chapter, I had the rare opportunity to participate in a service of Word and Sacrament in an assembly where I had not previously worshiped. The liturgy was carefully crafted and shaped by the lections for this particular Sunday. The sermon exemplified what I am attempting to share in these reflections. What became a gospel moment happened during the distribution of the bread and wine as the pianist played an improvisation on the American folk tune NETTLETON. I found myself silently singing, "Come, Thou Fount of Every Blessing," and I could hear a person sitting behind me very quietly humming the hymn. It truly was what someone would consider "traveling music," as the assembly moved forward to receive the bread and cup that became a gospel encounter. Hymns, even when there are no words attached to the music, gospel. J. S. Bach composed forty-six chorale preludes on German hymn-tunes. They were not intended for organ concerts but for the liturgy, to provide an organ setting of a hymn the assembly would be singing in that liturgy. I always maintain that the music that is labeled as a "prelude" in the liturgy is part of the liturgy itself, not some "cover-up" for the chattering and other noises associated with an assembly's gathering.

The organist who serves with me frequently plays a prelude on the setting of a hymn-tune which is the same as the tune of the first hymn the assembly will sing. We solved the chatter problem by chiming the hour. The presider gives a brief greeting and any brief announcements—not a repetition of what is already printed in the bulletin! Then the presider says, "Let us worship God as _____ (acolyte) brings in the light of Christ, and _____ (organist) leads us into _____ (the Sunday in the church year)." This makes the prelude, accompanied by the nonverbal lighting of the candles, as truly the initial liturgical actions that are part of the *ordo*'s "Gathering."

Human life always is lived between the "already" and the "not yet." Often the dichotomy is spoken of as the times between the past and the future as measured by clocks and calendars. Yet, from a biblical perspective the in-between-ness is what God is doing between what God has already done and what God will yet do in God's time (*kairos* rather than *chronos*). W. G. Kümmel more than fifty years ago titled his book on Jesus's eschatological message, *Promise and Fulfillment*.[1] More on this will be the focus of the last chapter. Worship is the praxis of this in-between-ness between God's promise and God's fulfillment, and liturgically it has been expressed in the ancient eucharistic affirmation, "Christ has died, Christ is risen, Christ will come again." So, to preach evangelically is to gospel the in-between-ness of God and invite an assembly into God's "already" and "not yet," into what God is doing in that in-between-ness in the world, church, and their individual lives. To gospel the in-between-ness is to let the light of Christ shine through the windows of worship to illuminate, through the Holy Spirit, what God is doing *now* between God's promise and God's fulfillment. The power is the Spirit at work through the Word, not the eloquence or persuasiveness of the preacher. The assembly's discovery individually and corporately of what God is doing is not to be programmed or controlled. To gospel, homiletically and liturgically, is to let God be God and to let the mystery of God "who moves in a mysterious way" perform God's wonders. Every Lord's Day is Easter, but every Lord's Day is also

1. Werner Georg Kümmel, *Promise and Fulfillment: The Eschatological Message of Jesus*, trans. Dorothea M. Barton (London: SCM, 1957).

Advent: "Christ is risen" and "Christ is coming." And to gospel is to *announce* what God is doing *between* Easter and Advent, not just as seasons in the church year, but as "already" and "not yet" *kairoi* in God's time. The Greek verb form is *angelizō*, "announce." Allied with *angelizō* is the noun, *angelos*, "angel," "messenger." How often are mortals in the Bible touched by angel/messengers announcing that something good is happening or going to happen? In Baroque churches somehow angels choose trumpets to do their announcing.

The metaphor of the herald is the image in days before mass media and even before universal literacy of the town crier standing on the town green heralding, "Hear, ye! Hear, ye!" Think of what it meant when Independence in the American colonies was declared, not just as a document, but as it was verbally articulated! To herald "Hear, ye!" presupposed an assembly of hearers—more of which will be addressed in the next chapter. And "hearing" is more than an auditory function. "Hear, ye!" is meant to prompt listening. Many New England meeting houses were constructed on the public town green, the same place where the town crier announced the news. Obviously the situating of churches on town greens was part of the New England construct of social, religious, and political life. Yet, the metaphor of the church being at the place of announcing is meaningful.

A second-career pastor was called at her ordination to a church that had the marks of a dying congregation. The church building was a less-than-well-cared-for early nineteenth-century edifice surrounded on three sides by an ancient cemetery and fronted by a busy state highway. Its cemetery setting seemed to match its future. It is in the center of that village, yes, but it neither announces itself nor even says "hello." Yet within five years of the arrival of this new pastor, over two hundred people united with this congregation. Two hundred new members in five years would make anybody in the church-growth movement listen up! I asked, "Sara, what's your secret?" Her response was simply, "I preach the gospel, and I love the people."

"To gospel" in that congregation, to announce what God

is doing, is what lies at the root of preaching evangelically—announcing good news lovingly. The Greek prefix is *eu*, as in *euangelizō*, and it means "good," and there are a number of English words that begin with "eu." So, because in English we lack a verb for "gospel," we have to invent one: "gospel" as a verb. The Greek verb *euangelizō* means literally "to announce good," good news, the good news of God. Now that's hardly something new to folks who have been around church for a long time. However, to folks who haven't been around church for a while or even ever, "to gospel" connotes "to scold," "to make feel guilty," "to frighten," and any other announcement of the "bad." Admittedly there are many bad-sounding texts in the Bible, and there are some sermonizers who feast homiletically on those texts, and there are a lot of sermons delivered regularly only on Old Testament judgment texts. Even those of us who follow the discipline of the lectionary encounter texts that startle the preacher: "Oh my God, what am I going to do with *that*?"

The line—sometimes a fine one—between what is good news and what is perceived as bad news lies in the way in which the gospel is gospeled. I remember Sara's response: "I preach the gospel and love the people." Those are not two separate actions, and Sara's "love the people" is not some kind of valentine schmaltz. I will speak more about preaching contextually in the next chapter, but gospeling the gospel lovingly is at the heart of preaching evangelically. It is an *art* that demands careful attention and practice to announce a gospel that is both judgment and grace in such a way that the preacher neither tries to play God nor is perceived as being God. God is love, and that love is both judgment and grace. So the awesome task of preaching evangelically is to gospel a love in which also God's judgment is heard. The biblical text is part of that which is the "already" in which God has spoken. What God will speak and what God will do is the "not yet." Preaching evangelically is inviting the assembly into that in-between-ness. And if God's love stings and bites as judgment on individuals and societies, let the judgment be *God's* Word. The giftedness of Martin Luther

King as a preacher was his ability to engage people lovingly into a text and to let the fiery judgment of God fall on all those with ears to hear.

This past Sunday, as of this writing, the Gospel text was the parable in Matthew of the unforgiving servant/slave. The final two verses read: "And in anger his lord handed him over to be tortured until he would pay his entire debt. So my heavenly Father will also do to every one of you, if you do not forgive your brother or sister from your heart" (Matt. 18:34–35). Could I, should I, would I, have said in the sermon, "If you don't forgive your brother or sister from your heart, God, like the angry king, will torture you"? If I had, I would have been playing God. The preacher is not the judge. Only God will do what God will do.

Instead, I tried to invite the assembly into the in-between-ness of an ancient text—with the idiosyncrasies unique to the writer of Matthew's Gospel—and the "not-yet-ness" of judgment that rests in the mind of God. I juxtaposed this text with the Lukan version of the Lord's Prayer, which this congregation prays weekly: "and forgive us our sins as we forgive those who sin against us." And, without saying so, I left the judgment of those who cannot forgive those who sin against them up to God.

I ended the sermon with a true story of two brothers. The setting was Bixler's Hardware Store in Carlisle, Pennsylvania. It prided itself on being "the second-oldest hardware store in the USA" and was situated on a corner of the public square. Unfortunately Bixler's is no more. At the back of the store Woody and John held court behind the counter at the cash register. There were some benches where some of the locals would sit and catch up on the latest gossip. One day an elderly farmer was sitting there chatting with John and Woody. All at once another elderly man came in and sat down, whereupon the first one immediately, without a word, got up and walked out. John said to the newly arrived one, "Wasn't that your brother?" "Yeah, but we haven't spoken to each other ever since we were teenagers and had a fight over whose pig it was that won a ribbon at the county fair." My last words of the sermon were: "I assume that they both are dead now, and I keep wondering whether the brothers ever broke the hostile silence and spoke a forgiving word with each other—before one of them died. 'Forgive us our sins, as we forgive those who sin against us.'" I left whatever judgment would be rendered in sacramental silence.

To preach evangelically is to preach *prophetically*. Much has been written about "prophetic preaching," which, depending on the theological mindset of the writer, can range from predictions of the end-time to the latest "hot-button" cultural issue. Leonora Tubbs Tisdale in a chapter titled "What Is Prophetic Preaching?" says, "'Prophetic' is currently used in church circles in ways that can be confusing and even conflicting."[2] In some assemblies prophetic preaching on social-issue topics is encouraged; in others it becomes warrant for the preacher's dismissal. Tisdale suggests several approaches offered by a variety of preachers and theologians. She quotes one suggested by Philip Wogaman in his book *Speaking Truth in Love: Prophetic Preaching in a Broken World*: "To be prophetic," Wogaman said, "is not necessarily to be adversarial, or even controversial. The word in its Greek form refers to one who speaks on behalf of another. In Hebrew tradition, a prophet is one who 'speaks for God.' . . . Genuine prophetic preaching draws people into the reality of God in such a way that they cannot any longer be content with conventional wisdom and superficial existence."[3]

Wogaman's definition, to me, pushes "prophetic" as an adjective into the adverb "prophetically." This means that gospeling prophetically actively invites an assembly into an engagement, a happening, of the word of God. Preaching prophetically—"speaking *for* God"—creates a homiletical and liturgical window through which *God* speaks, and the focus is not on the preacher and the issues but on the divine Speaker so that, in

2. Leonora Tubbs Tisdale, *Prophetic Preaching: A Pastoral Approach* (Louisville: Westminster John Knox, 2010), 3.

3. Quoted in Tisdale, *Prophetic Preaching*, 3, from Philip Wogaman, *Speaking Truth in Love: Prophetic Preaching in a Broken World* (Louisville: Westminster John Knox, 1998), 3.

the metaphors of the biblical prophets themselves, "The Word of God came to [comes to] . . ."

Before the reading of Scripture and the preaching of the sermon the lector in the church I serve always prays a prayer for illumination followed by the charge: "Listen *for* the Word of God." To listen *for* is more than to listen *to*. To listen *to* the Word of God is passively to hear words with meanings encapsulated in ancient texts as though God had nothing more to say after the canon of the Bible was closed. To listen *for*, on the other hand, is an invitation into a gospel that opens in the "in-between-ness" of what God has done and what God will do, or in Jesus's hermeneutic: "Today this scripture has been fulfilled *in your hearing.*" The intent of "fulfilled in your hearing" is both an individual and corporate invitation into a divine Word of judgment and grace that, through the Holy Spirit, is happening *now.*

Yet, God's *now* is not frozen in the present moment. God's *now* has an open-ended-ness that pushes what God is doing now into the future tense: what God *will do.* Preaching prophetically and evangelically requires the art of what Walter Brueggemann calls "the prophetic imagination." "Prophetic ministry," he maintains, "consists of offering an alternative perception of reality and in letting people see their own history in light of God's freedom and his will for justice. [These] issues are not always and need not be expressed primarily in the big issues of the day. They can be discerned wherever people try to live together."[4] He asserts, "The formation of an alternative community with an alternative consciousness is so that the dominant community may be criticized and finally dismantled. But, more than dismantling, the purpose of the alternative community is to enable a new human beginning to be made."[5]

One of the lectionary-appointed texts for Easter 5 in year B is the story of the encounter between Philip and the Ethiopian

---

4. Walter Brueggemann, *The Prophetic Imagination* (Philadelphia: Fortress, 1978), 116.
5. Brueggemann, *The Prophetic Imagination*, 96.

eunuch in Acts 8:26–40. It is not one of those "Thus says the Lord" kinds of texts generally associated with prophetic voices. Yet, the text itself prophetically raises the contemporary question of inclusivity as the eunuch asks Philip: "What is to prevent me from being baptized?" (Acts 8:36). Preaching prophetically is allowing the text itself to raise the question homiletically so that those who have ears to hear, again in Wogaman's words, "cannot any longer be content with conventional wisdom and superficial existence."

During the past half century I have presided, preached, or attended many funerals and many so-called "memorial services." The word "memorial" reveals the underlying paradigm—to remember the deceased. The word for such memorializing is to "eulogize," that is, to speak a "good word" about the character and deeds of the deceased. It is the custom in some traditions to invite anyone who wishes to come to a microphone and say good words about the one who died. The net result is a ritual of eulogizing, good words about the deceased, and very little gospeling of the good news of Christ's victory over the powers of sin and death and the promise of resurrection for those who live and die in Christ. Perhaps in my dotage I have become a cynic, but too often I have to listen hard to hear at least a snippet of gospel in the midst of endless eulogies. The occasion of the gathering of an assembly for one who has died is truly a time to gospel the great mystery of Christ and to invite those who mourn to be immersed, nonjudgmentally, in the promises of God that lead from death to new life. In some African American congregations such celebrations are called "going home" services.

President Obama in June of 2015 was called upon to offer a eulogy for the senior pastor of Emanuel AME Church in Charleston, South Carolina, state senator Clementa C. Pinckney, and eight members of the church who, while engaged in a Bible study session, were gunned down by a white supremacist. The President's eulogizing followed the traditional themes of extolling the virtues of the deceased pastor and members of the congregation. Yet, after a while it became apparent to me that

President Obama was moving into gospeling justice and the eschatological promises of a God "who moves in mysterious ways his wonders to perform." He was not simply eulogizing the dead but preaching what God was doing amidst the horror of the shooting. And he ended by starting to sing, "Amazing grace, how sweet the sound," and the whole assembly began to join him, "that saved a wretch like me. I once was lost, but now am found, was blind, but now I see." All of a sudden the metaphors in John Newton's famous hymn took on gospel meaning in that moment, and the personal pronouns of the hymn homiletically and liturgically became the "we's" of everyone in that assembly and those around the world who were watching—and perhaps singing along. It was truly a moment of gospeling that took on sacramental dimensions. Yet, the sad thing was that the media and much of the general public had no clue that the President was preaching! The media pundits and Washington politicians turned it into political rhetoric.

Of course, in such a public setting the other half of a memorial service of worship—the eucharist—was missing. I will share more in the final chapter about the celebration of the eucharist in a funeral or memorial service. Suffice it to say here that Protestants generally have excised from this end-of-life thanksgiving what has been normative in some other Christian traditions. After I had sung many classic requiem masses as concert pieces, it dawned on me that these were not just designed as musical performances, but as musical settings of the order for the memorializing of the deaths of individuals, and, as in the case of Benjamin Britten's *War Requiem*, performed at the dedication of the new Coventry Cathedral in England in memory of those who lost their lives in the firebombings of World War II. Why should we exclude eucharist from the funerals for the less than famous?

There is in my mind a huge theological error, particularly in some Reformed circles, that holy communion is restricted to Maundy Thursday, and that Easter is the day for eggs, bunnies, and pageants of an empty tomb. The empty-tomb-ness of many Easter worship services, even though the church is gloriously festooned with memorial lilies, reveals leaders' ignorance of the Scriptures or pure prejudice against things "liturgical." Unfortunately some preachers are hard pressed to say anything that resembles a gospeling of the resurrection victory or to encourage congregations to step out of the empty tombs of their Easter traditions into a eucharistic celebration of the real presence of the risen Christ. To gospel Easter is to gospel in Word *and* Sacrament.

I encouraged one congregation on the front range of the Rocky Mountains to transform their traditional "Easter Dawn Service" into a celebration of the Great Vigil of Easter, one of the oldest liturgical traditions. The service begins out of doors with the lighting of a new fire and the passing of the light of Christ to individual candles in the predawn darkness, continues with the reading of Old Testament lections, and when possible the celebration of baptism. The centerpiece is the gospel acclamation: "The Lord is risen!" to which the assembly shouts, "He is risen indeed!" accompanied by the ringing of bells and beating of drums. The service concludes with the eucharist. As the assembly there in the meditation-glen/columbarium in the shadows of Pike's Peak gathered at the outdoor table to receive the bread and wine of the eucharist, the sun rose over the Colorado plains from the East. "The Lord is risen!" "He is risen indeed!" received nature's accompaniment! The Great Vigil demands no special technologies—simply candles, bread, and wine—to gospel Easter's resurrection. It doesn't even need a church building!

Although Easter from the beginning has been the centerpiece of the church's gospeling, each Lord's Day, each Sunday, is Easter all over again. Even the counting of the forty days of Lent from Ash Wednesday through Holy Saturday excludes Sundays. They are little Easters, and the other forty days of Lent wrap themselves around the Easters. Preaching evangelically is to gospel each Sunday in Word and Sacrament with the good news of what God is doing in the midst of a world of pain and joy and in the context of each assembly gathered under the Word of God.

5

Preaching *Contextually*

"Let anyone with ears to hear listen!"

—Mark 4:9; 4:23; Luke 8:8; 14:35

"Let anyone who has an ear listen to what the Spirit is saying to the churches."

—Revelation 2:7; 2:11; 2:17; 2:29; 3:6; 3:13; 3:22

Twice in Mark's Gospel and twice in Luke's, Jesus is quoted as a conclusion to a parable or a saying, "Let anyone with ears to hear listen!" Each of the risen Christ's messages to the seven churches in the Apocalypse of John ends with: "Let anyone who has an ear listen to what the Spirit is saying to the churches." Obviously, these repetitions in Scripture reveal that these exhortations already were part of the liturgical life of the church before their inclusion in what eventuated as the New Testament. Liturgically they lend themselves presumably to conclusions to the readings of Scripture.

Homiletically, they also presume that there are "hearers" of what is spoken. Of course, "ears" and "hear" are not anatomical body parts and audiological functions but metaphors of the reception of what is gospeled. Hence, they are not restricted to what occurs or doesn't occur when an audiologist tests someone's hearing. Rather, "hearing" is that which is effected through the Holy Spirit's action in the sacramental transaction between what is gospeled and what is perceived by the hearers. In the opening chapter we were confronted by Paul's rhetorical question in the letter to the Romans: "And how shall they hear without a preacher?" (Rom. 10:14 KJV). We now reverse the question, "How can a preacher preach without hearers?" The primary locus of preaching contextually is "hearers." It is among the hearers that the Holy Spirit speaks. And again, "hearer" is not restricted to the ability or inability to process sounds. The Holy Spirit speaks sometimes in "sighs too deep for words" and sometimes in "clanging bells and crashing cymbals," all of which say, "Listen up!"

Legend has it that in the thirteenth century Francis of Assisi preached to anyone who had ears to hear, even to the birds. Sometimes I wonder whether some of my sermons have been, jokingly, "for the birds"! I have preached outdoors to the accompaniment of squawking swans and geese and indoors as a Christmas-eve lamb bleated into my cordless microphone. I have had to compete homiletically with crying babies and octogenarians with screeching hearing aids. I have preached in the National Cathedral in Washington, DC, and in a tiny chapel in the Appalachian mountains of Pennsylvania. I have preached in Cuban churches where every word of mine had to be translated into Spanish, and I have preached in German to congregations in the former "Eastern Zone" of Germany. I have preached in assemblies that have been numbered in the hundreds and others less than a dozen. I have preached in prison cell-blocks and in seminary chapels. I have preached in nursing homes where many in the assembly were sound asleep before and after the sermon, and I have preached in assemblies of children overdosed on Easter candy. And, each time, preaching contextually always asks: Who are the hearers? And what is heard?

I once preached what I thought was the sermon of all sermons that would convince everyone of the immorality of the war in Vietnam. Hazel, a proper woman who always addressed me as "Mr. Mitman," commented as I greeted her at the door,

"Mr. Mitman, that sermon was wonderful. It convinced me more and more that we need to stay in Vietnam and fight it out to the end!" Hazel had good ears to hear and a sharp mind to process the information her ears were hearing. However, was the Holy Spirit saying another word to her than the words that were coming from my mouth? That moment has humbled me for the rest of my life, for in the words of the old Scottish hymn—pardon the noninclusive language—"God is his own interpreter, and he will make it plain."

American religious individualism is not helped by the lack of a separate word for the second person plural in contemporary English usage. In earlier English usages, such as in the King James Bible and Shakespeare's writings, the singulars *thee* (nominative), *thou* (objective), and *thine* (possessive) were distinguished from the plural *ye* (nominative) and *you* (objective). So, when sixteenth-century English ears heard, "Ye are the salt of the earth," it was clear that Jesus's saying in the King James translation of Matthew 5:13 was meant plurally. Likewise in the King James translation of John 1:26, "John [the Baptist] answered them, saying, I baptize with water: but there standeth one among you, whom ye know not." "You" is the objective plural, and "ye" is the nominative plural. Contemporary English has obliterated the grammatical distinctions, and "you" is both singular and plural, nominative and objective, and "your" is the possessive, both singular and plural. Twenty-first-century ears hear the texts very differently from those of the sixteenth century or from those, even today, who hear these texts in languages with different words for the singulars and plurals, and, of course, different words for the grammatical cases of the pronouns. Having preached in German, I am convinced that German ears hear these texts differently, hopefully more collectively, than we Americans hear. When the New England town crier yelled, "Hear ye, hear ye," it was clear that the hearing was intended to be by more than a solitary individual. The art of preaching contextually in today's American society is increasingly more difficult without ears attuned to hearing corporately.

Gordon Lathrop in *Holy People: A Liturgical Ecclesiology* writes,

The prophets and apostles were speaking to assemblies. Christians dare to let their current gatherings listen as if they were in continuity with those ancient assemblies. What is more, the Jesus of the New Testament stories was already gathering a collection of people around him in his ministry, and the present assembly for worship does intend to continue the religiously revolutionary business of those old gatherings around him. In fact, the only stories of Jesus that we have are stories that were collected and told in *churches*, for the purposes of the faith alive in those churches. Furthermore, if an individual hears the Scripture freshly, what he or she hears does need to be told to the assembly. Finally, Christians believe that the Word of God calls us into assembly. "Assembly" is found throughout the pages of the Scriptures, and assembly continues to be the context in which we receive the Scriptures today.[1]

Although "congregation" and "congregational" are part of my own ecclesiastical tradition, I have stopped using "congregation" homiletically and liturgically. I use "assembly" instead. "Congregation" infers a kind of elitism, a clubbish "in" group who have signed the membership book and who contribute. Many church bylaws define "membership" as those who attend, contribute, and commune—at least once yearly. And provisions exist for those who don't to be "erased." I have fifty years of horrible stories of self-righteous elders, pastors, and even church secretaries, who delighted in "cleaning out the membership rolls." There still are ecclesiastical traditions that practice "fenced tables," that is, to them holy communion is a "members only" meal, and decisions as to who may receive the bread and cup are defined either by canon law or determined by proper clerical and lay authorities. In my own tradition it

1. Gordon W. Lathrop, *Holy People: A Liturgical Ecclesiology* (Minneapolis: Fortress, 1999), 25.

was the practice for local church elders to determine the spiritual fitness of communicants and to give those deemed worthy a token for admission to the table—yes, like the tokens that before digitalized cards replaced them were put into machines to grant entry to subways and buses! I also do not use "member" except for necessary record-keeping. Membership lists are not the contexts for preaching; assemblies are. Assemblies gospel (verb); assemblies *do* liturgy.

Lathrop provides extensive background into the meaning of "assembly"—far more than I can cite here. He traces "assembly" in Greco-Roman social and religious life and in the gatherings of the early Christian communities. He continues,

> Christianity widely called itself not "club" or *collegium*, but "the meeting" or "the assembly"—*ekklēsia*, in Greek. . . . This Greek word—*ekklēsia*—is the one we customarily translate in English and in other German and Slavic languages as "church" (or *kirche, kyrka, kerk, cirkev*), and . . . we need to read "assembly" wherever our languages say "church" or *iglesia*. Unlike the clubs [of the Hellenistic world], the Christians were "the assembly," "the meeting," all of the time. They took this word as the name of their group.[2]

And by the time the New Testament came into being, *ekklēsia* had assumed not only local gatherings but also the idea of a worldwide assembly.

Although Paul gospeled in nonecclesial and civil contexts (for example, at the Areopagus in Athens), and although gospelers have gospeled in a myriad of contexts through the centuries, the dominant setting has been in the *ekklēsia*—construed in the widest sense both locally and far beyond the walls of individual "church" buildings. Colonial New England "meeting houses" often were erected on public squares and were used for civic and even political gatherings. Nevertheless, their primary purpose was to house the "assembly," the church. And in

2. Lathrop, *Holy People*, 30–31.

much of the public mind today preaching is thought to be what happens "in church." Furthermore, when someone says, "I'm going to church," it may mean going to a specific building, but more fundamentally means, "I'm going to an assembly" where something is supposed to happen. Preaching contextually in present-day American society is primarily related to the "outpost of human hurts and hopes" (Kennon Callahan) of a specific assembly that is expected to show up in a certain place on a Sunday morning. And in most traditional settings if a foot of snow is dumped from the skies on a Saturday night or a hurricane or tornado blows through with 100-plus mile-per-hour winds, and if a notice appears on the congregation's website, "Church is canceled today," does that mean that the "assembly" doesn't exist that day? Hardly. Unless the roof blows off—and maybe even if it does—the assembly will "have church" come next Sunday. Contextually the gospeler(s) on that next Sunday must gospel the goodness of God in the midst of the assembly's tragedy. (I rarely use the word "must!)

By the way, I continue to be amazed that after the tragedy of 9/11, many churches the next Sunday went about business as usual as though nothing had happened! I was in York, England, where I watched on British TV as the towers of the World Trade Center fell. Within a few hours, the daily-appointed evensong began in York Minster cathedral. The context of what happens every afternoon in that great cathedral had changed, and within hours of the tragedy the preaching and prayers reflected that the world had been plunged into a new era in little more than a twinkling of an eye. And if the leadership of that assembly had closed their homiletical and liturgical eyes and continued with business as usual, that appointed hour would have been a sham.

In 1963 *Time* magazine published a piece on Swiss theologian Karl Barth who said that forty years earlier "he advised young theologians 'to take your Bible and take your newspaper, and read both. But interpret newspapers from your Bible.'"[3]

3. *Time*, Friday, May 31, 1963.

Variations on this theme of Barth have recontextualized themselves worldwide for nearly a century. In his commentary on Romans, first published in 1922 and which marked a turning point in German theology, Barth said that "the reading of all sorts of decidedly secular literature, above all the newspaper, is urgently recommended in order to understand the Letter to the Romans."[4] The same *Time* article comments on Barth's insistence on the importance of newspapers: "Newspapers . . . are so important that 'I always pray for the sick, the poor, journalists, authorities of the state and the church—in that order. Journalists form public opinion. They hold terribly important positions.'" I wonder what Barth would say today when most people do not read newspapers but get information electronically from television, the Internet, social media, and even bloggers! In an era of post-facticity we need more than ever fact-checkers to help us discern truth from falsehood. I still read newspapers. By Sunday morning the weekly sermon has been manuscripted, and as I eat breakfast I scan the newspaper in the hopes that within a few hours I will be preaching in an assembly on a text of Scripture contextually and contemporaneously.

Yet, it is not the context itself that determines gospeling. Barth's instruction to preachers to read both newspapers and the Bible is coupled with: "But interpret newspapers from your Bible." Since Barth first gave that advice, there has been an eruption of biblical fundamentalism that would "interpret newspapers from your Bible" in a literal and legalistic sense, giving preachers license to promulgate a particular ideological or even political spin on world events with the justification, "The Bible says so." Such talk is abusive and frightening. Gospeling contextually involves a hopefully more humble hermeneutic, as I tried to approach in previous chapters.

When I was an undergraduate and still less than two decades old, I first encountered Douglas Horton's translation of Barth's *Das Wort Gottes und die Theologie*, strangely translated as

---

4. From Princeton Theological Seminary Library Homepage, translation mine.

The Word of God and the Word of Man.[5] As I open that collection of Barth's speeches, I find words that I underlined more than a half-century ago. (It is impossible to reduce Barth to snippets of quotes, so here's the whole thing!) It is translated from an address titled "The Strange New World in the Bible" that Barth spoke to the church at Lentwil, Switzerland, in the autumn of 1916.

> Ere long the Bible says to us . . . "These may be you, but they are not I! They may perhaps suit you, meeting the demands of your thought and temperament, of your era and your 'circle,' of your religious or philosophical theories. You wanted to be mirrored in me, and now you have really found in me your own reflection. But now I bid you come seek *me*, as well. Seek what is here." . . . There is a river in the Bible that carries us away, once we have entrusted our destiny to it—away from ourselves to the sea. The Holy Scriptures will interpret themselves in spite of all our human limitations. We need only dare to follow this drive, this spirit, this river, to grow out beyond ourselves toward the highest answer. This daring is *faith*; and we read the Bible rightly, not when we do so with false modesty, restraint, and attempted sobriety, for these are passive qualities, but when we read it in faith. And the invitation to dare and to reach toward the highest, even though we do not deserve it, is the expression of *grace* in the Bible: the Bible unfolds to us as we are met, guided, drawn on, and made to grow by the grace of God.[6]

In the same address Barth continues:

> Once more we stand before this "other" new world which begins in the Bible. In it the chief consideration is not the doings of [human beings] but the doings of God—not the

---

5. Karl Barth, *The Word of God and the Word of Man*, trans. Douglas Horton (New York: Harper & Brothers, 1956).
6. Barth, *The Word of God and the Word of Man*, 33–34.

various ways which we may take if we are [people] of good will, but the power out of which good will must first be created—not the unfolding and fruition of love as we may understand it, but the existence and outpouring of eternal love, of love as God understands it—not industry, honesty, and helpful as we may practice them in our old ordinary world, but the establishment and growth of a new world, the world in which God and [God's] morality reign. . . . It is not the right thoughts about God which form the content of the Bible, but the right divine thoughts about [humankind]. The Bible tells us not how we should talk with God but what [God] says to us; not how we find the way to [God], but how [God] has sought and found the way to us; not the right relations in which we must place ourselves to [God], but the covenant which [God] has made with all who are Abraham's spiritual children and which [God] has sealed once and for all in Jesus Christ. It is this which is within the Bible. The word of God is within the Bible.[7]

Note the preposition "within." The Word of God is textualized *within* the Bible, textualized by those who in faith passed on the Word of God, and the Word of God is contextualized in the church's gospeling of the Word of God. Yes, the Word of God is spoken in the context of human experience, but it is not human experience that determines the content of the gospeling. Bishop William H. Willimon once wrote, "The gospel is an intrusion among us, not something arising out of us. . . . I don't preach Jesus' story in the light of my experience, as some sort of helpful symbol or myth that is usefully illumined by my story. Rather, I am invited by Easter to interpret my story in the light of God's triumph in the resurrection."[8] Although Willimon was speaking in the first person singular, his testimony can be expanded to say that in the gospeling event

---

7. Barth, *The Word of God and the Word of Man*, 39, 43.
8. William H. Willimon, *The Intrusive Word: Preaching to the Unbaptized* (Grand Rapids: Eerdmans, 1994), 25.

the whole assembly is invited by Easter to interpret *their* story, individually and corporately, in the light of God's triumph in the resurrection of Jesus Christ. And, further, it is the whole assembly—those appointed to preside (that is, literally, to "sit up front") as well as those who find it more comfortable to sit in the pews and do liturgy—to be invited together to be addressed by the Word of God that intrudes into the midst of the assembly with an Easter surprise.

In 1935 Barth prepared a lecture titled "Gospel and Law," which was supposed to be delivered at a conference in Barmen, Germany, but he was prohibited from doing so by Hitler's Gestapo. Consequently it was delivered by another person, and Barth was quickly escorted across the border to Switzerland by the German police. His reversal of the traditional duality of "law and gospel" is intentional:

> The Word of God is the one "Word of truth. . . . The Word of God, when it is addressed to us and when we are allowed to hear it, demonstrates its unity in that it is always *grace*; i.e., it is free, non-obligatory, undeserved divine goodness, mercy, and condescension. A Gospel or a Law which we speak to ourselves, by virtue of our own ability and trusting in our own authority and credibility, would, as such not be *God's* Word; it would not be *his* Gospel and it would not be *his* law. The *very fact that* God speaks to us, that, under all circumstances, is, in itself, grace. . . . Precisely because the *Gospel* has grace as its *particular direct* content, which then also includes, in itself, the content of the Law, it enforces its *priority* over the Law which still, included in the Gospel and relative to it, is no less God's Word.[9]

A year earlier, May 29–31, 1934, those who opposed Hitler's takeover of the German Protestant Church had gathered in Bar-

9. Karl Barth, *Community, State, and Church: Three Essays by Karl Barth*, ed. Will Herberg, trans. G. Ronald Howe (Garden City, NY: Anchor/Doubleday, 1960), 72–73.

men. Barth was the penman of what eventuated as the "Barmen Declaration" of the Confessing Church. It begins, "Jesus Christ, as he is attested to us in Holy Scripture, is the one Word of God whom we have to hear, and whom we have to trust and obey in life and in death. We reject the false doctrine that the Church could and should recognize as a source of its proclamation, beyond and besides this one Word of God, yet other events, powers, historic figures and truths as God's revelation." The contexts of Germany—and the world, for that matter—during the rise and fall of the Hitler regime ooze out from the edges of Barth's writing and preaching. Yet, it is never those contexts, as the Barmen Declaration testifies, that determine the content. The gospel is Jesus Christ, the one Word of God. And the proclamation of the one Word of God is both gospel and law, grace and judgment. Those who allow a lectionary to shape an assembly's worship find themselves engaged each week liturgically and homiletically with both law and gospel through at least four Old and New Testament texts and Psalms—all of which *together* are vessels for God's Word to become, through the one Word, Jesus Christ, enfleshed in those who have ears to hear.

For eighteen years of my ministry each Sunday I found myself present, presiding, or preaching in one or more of 175 churches in southeastern Pennsylvania. Preaching contextually was made more difficult in that, although I knew who the leaders were and something about the location of each church, sometimes the purpose for my being in that particular church was that there was either a celebration or a problem. Yet, being the unrepentant lectionary preacher that I am, I insisted—generally—on preaching the lectionary texts. It was also part of my pastoral and teaching responsibility to prepare the liturgy for and to preside and preach in monthly services of Word and Sacrament in the Conference's Church House chapel. These liturgies and sermons were shaped by texts appointed in the Revised Common Lectionary for several weeks in advance, and the assembly generally was a group of pastors and parish musicians. I soon discovered that I could not "repreach" the same sermon in one of the churches. The texts were the same, but the contexts were totally different. I do have an electronic "barrel" of sermons for every Sunday in the liturgical year in the three-year cycle, but barreled sermons are not like vintage wine that gets better with age. Sermons sour quickly even on a flash drive!

Preaching contextually raises the larger question of the cultural contexts in which gospeling occurs. In a volume titled *Worship and Culture: Foreign Country or Homeland?*, Dr. Gláucia Vasconcelos Wilkey has brought together, from an ecumenical perspective, a collection of essays by various writers on the subject of worship and culture throughout the world. Reflecting on insights of the 1996 "Nairobi Statement on Worship and Culture: Contemporary Challenges and Opportunities," Gordon Lathrop writes, "Christian worship is marked by a transcultural, contextual, cross-cultural, and countercultural relationship to every culture. All four. Gathered around a few transcultural central things—important to us because of their association with Jesus as well as their long centrality in Christian practice—Christian liturgy [in which, in my mind, preaching as gospeling is integral] seeks to arrive in every cultural place, welcoming local and distant, contextual and cross-cultural gifts into its hybrid practice, while it also seeks to resist the dangerous, sometimes murderous, practices of local cultures, including especially their practices of identity purity."[10] The latter evokes images of attempts at ethnic and religious cleansing that result in the willful murder of, for example, Coptic Christians in Egypt, or ISIS's killing and chasing hundreds of thousands of Orthodox Christians from their homes in Syria. The numbers of "murderous practices of local cultures" are too frightening to count, and even "unpure" Muslims are not exempt. Yet, homegrown attempts to be more religiously pure right here in my neighborhood spawn more and more groups bent on enforcing their own brands of religious—and even political—orthodoxy.

---

10. Gordon W. Lathrop, "Every Foreign Country a Homeland, Every Homeland a Foreign Country," in *Worship and Culture*, ed. Gláucia Vasconcelos Wilkey (Grand Rapids: Eerdmans, 2014), 22.

In the same volume Dirk Lange explains that

> worship and culture are not two distinct entities; rather, they are codependent and cannot be thought of separately. The relationships of worship and culture imply organic, material, earthy, incarnational dimensions—the complexity of living things, not static entities. Neat categorization becomes impossible. . . . Worship is a peculiar form of translation. It is the translation, not of an original idea, or work, or doctrine, but of an event that is never captured in its happening. Worship as translation is itself a living event. Worship arises out of that demand to say the "unsayable," to express the inexpressible, to name what is impossible to name, what always remains inaccessible, intangible in an event. . . . Worship, then, is not simply translating a pattern into various contexts: rather, within each context, in all the multicultural characteristics of each context, worship registers the force of an experience, the dynamic of the gospel, the continual return and irruption of the Holy Spirit. . . . The rituals of worship and their ordering are not tools for the mastery of Christian life but rather an incessant questioning: How does the gospel, the Christ event, become for us?[11]

He continues:

> A concept can be neatly explained; the living tension in word and body cannot. Word and sacrament are not transcultural entities, but are living things happening in the midst of an assembled people. They are made alive—that is, they are "living things" by action of the Holy Spirit alone, who is continually interpreting anew God's promise in every context. . . . Word and sacrament are constantly opening up a worshiping assembly, a faith community, to what cannot be captured, verified, represented within its midst—or within

11. Dirk G. Lange, "Worship: Translating the Untranslatable," in Vasconcelos Wilkey, *Worship* and *Culture*, 163–64.

its society and culture. . . . The liturgy is translated in such a way that the Spirit is continually interpreting context and culture and pushing it toward the gospel, that is, disrupting in what we might call a countercultural move.[12]

Many of the religious upstarts focus their ardor on addressing supposed religious help for personal problems. Faith in God solves problems. Slick postcards arrive in my mailbox regularly from some of these groups—they rarely use the word "church"—trying to promote programs for personal fulfillment and solving family and other interpersonal problems. There never is an invitation into the holy mysteries—not even in the cards arriving in Holy Week!

In North American culture there is an increasing number of those who have become identified as the "nones." These are those in the population who, when asked what their religious preference or affiliation is, mark "none." The Rev. Lillian Daniel, pastor of a large suburban Chicago congregation, has done research, writes books and articles, and lectures on this growing phenomenon, particularly about a certain segment of the nones, the SBNRs—the "Spiritual But Not Religious." In a recent study more than a third of the US population identified themselves as SBNRs. That percentage is doubled among those under thirty. Pastor Daniel's book, *When "Spiritual But Not Religious" Is Not Enough*,[13] provides a collection of engaging homilies/ sermons that address both the church and those discovering that SBNR is not enough, from the perspective of the gospel and the church's proclamation of the gospel in these days. Her homiletical style is both a pattern for the church and an invitation to those searching for something more. It is a bridge asking for conversations.

Every so often some of those nones, even the more "spiritual but not religious" ones, appear in a Christian assembly

---

12. Lange, "Worship: Translating the Untranslatable," 169–70.
13. Lillian Daniel, *When "Spiritual But Not Religious" Is Not Enough* (New York: Jericho Books, 2013).

gathered to do what it does generally on Sunday mornings—or at more culturally accommodating times. They appear sometimes for funerals or memorial services because somehow they are related to the deceased by family or friendship. Sometimes, too, for weddings, if they are "spiritual" enough not to forgo the liturgical stuff and just show up for the reception! Generally the nones and SBNRs have no clue as to what is supposed to happen when that particular assembly gathers, especially since a significant percentage of the population in the USA under thirty have never even been inside a church, synagogue, or mosque. "Church" is a context that is foreign territory for the nones and SBNRs. They are clueless as to what is supposed to happen.

A pastor friend tells the story of a young couple planning their wedding. The pastor agreed to meet with them and said, "I'll meet you at the church [on a certain day and time]." He assumed they would come to his study, but after the appointed time came and went and there was still no sign of their presence, he started searching throughout the church. He found them sitting in semi-darkness in the back pew of the church. Obviously this was strange territory for the groom-to-be, and, as he fidgeted in that back pew, he apologetically asked the pastor, "But . . . what do you do in here?"

More has been publicized in print and by the media about what the church needs to do for the clueless than I want to discuss here. In the end, I believe, what happens in the assembly in the hearts and minds of the clueless is really not the product of evangelism strategies and techniques but the result of the intrusion of the Word of God in ways more mysterious than our imaginations can conjure up. Grace happens, and the ones who "once were far off have been brought near" (Eph. 2:13), and the promised gift of the Holy Spirit "is for you, for your children, and for all who are far away, everyone whom the Lord our God calls to him" (Acts 2:39). By the way, the book of Acts is all about what the Holy Spirit does with nones and SBNRs!

I learned to know a dean of a certain independent college-prep school who always seemed to know about some of the books I had read and the teachers who had been my mentors. I knew that he had a master of divinity degree from one of the "ivy league" seminaries, but nothing more. He was a classic SBNR in the days before Lillian Daniel went to seminary herself. A terrible automobile accident happened on the campus of this particular school, and one of the teenagers whose family was part of the church I was serving was killed instantly. The memorial service was held in the church, and I invited the dean to represent the school and to participate liturgically in the memorial service. The church was jammed full of teenagers, many of them probably from SBNR families.

In the weeks that followed the tragedy, the dean and his family started participating in Sunday worship. It was the custom from time to time to receive "new members"—a word I no longer use. The dean asked for a pastoral visit. I rang the doorbell, and before I could step inside, he said, "You think you have come here to talk about church membership. I want to talk about conversion, baptism, and ordination!" It had taken him more than a decade since his graduation from divinity school to discover that being an SBNR was not enough. On a Sunday in the midst of the assembly he and his two sons were baptized (his wife had been baptized earlier in her life). One of the deacons always teased me that I was so "messy" in administering the water of baptism. But I remember to this day the drops of water mingled with the tears running down his face and the sunlight streaming through the windows, turning those drops of baptismal water into showers of heaven's grace. By the way, he also was received into discernment for ministry and ultimately was ordained to a ministry of Word and Sacrament.

Later I learned that the drops of water at one person's baptism can be the occasion for water to be sprinkled on the whole assembly as a reminder of their own baptism and communally the sacrament that unites all the baptized in the one body of Christ. The practice is called asperges (sprinkling with water), and by now the church I serve knows that when there is an evergreen branch lying next to the bowl of the font they are going to get wet—not dowsed but dropped on with gentle reminders of their baptism—accompanied by the gospeling words, "Remember your baptism and give thanks," and each individual's response: "Amen." Initially the assembly seemed to be startled by the drops, but now asperges is greeted with gracious smiles and thankful amens. In the previously cited book *The Intrusive Word: Preaching to the Unbaptized*, William Willimon says,

> Throwing water on someone in a church is strange . . . reminding us in word and water of the odd way we get saved by this peculiar faith. We follow Jesus, not because it was our idea, or because we were searching for something in our lives, or because we made a study of all the world's great religions and decided that Christianity is the best. We are here because we have been encountered, assaulted, intruded upon. . . . Evangelism ["gospeling" according to my translation of *angelizō*] begins in the odd, disruptive experience of being encountered by the gospel. Because the gospel is a way of thinking and being in the world that does not come naturally, we must be born again, and again.[14]

In this book Willimon couples each chapter with a sermon to illustrate how the chapter is contextualized homiletically in an assembly of academics in a large university chapel. The words just cited come from a chapter titled "Preaching as Baptismal Encounter," and the accompanying sermon is "The God of Second Chance."

We return to the earlier question: What will be heard by those who have ears to hear? A Bible-lands travelogue about far-away places with strange-sounding names? A fiery tirade about the latest hot-button social issue? An entertaining monologue to win friends and influence people? An erudite speech about religion to its cultured despisers? Or, is it the hope that those who have ears to hear will hear what God is saying *now* in the context of an assembly who live and move and have their being in a particular time and place?

14. Willimon, *The Intrusive Word*, 34–35.

Norman Hjelm writes in the introduction to *Worship and Culture*: "Worship of the triune God—at all times and in every culture—is the heart of the church's life. And it demonstrates that worship and culture is not to be regarded as an ossified item in ecclesiastical archives. Rather, it is to be seen as a step in a never-ending journey. To relate the worship of God to the realities of culture and of particular cultures is a perennial task."[15] He quotes from the Chicago Statement of the Lutheran World Federation: "The challenge is to develop and use forms of worship which are both authentic to the Gospel and relevant to local cultural contexts."[16] That challenge is not only the domain of official church bodies, but it also is what runs in the back of every preacher and presider's mind as he or she faces the awesome responsibility of preparing to gospel the Word of God authentically in a unique assembly in a specific place and in a specific slice of historic time.

It took some deep soul-searching for me to be able to affirm to myself that mortal words somehow by sacramental grace through the Holy Spirit can become the word of God for those who have ears to hear, and even, that God will give ears to those who claim they have no ears or even do not want ears to hear what God is saying.

15. Norman A. Hjelm, "From the Past to the Future: The LWF [Lutheran World Federation] Study Series on Worship and Culture as Vision and Mission," in Wilkey, *Worship and Culture*, 8.

16. Hjelm, "From the Past to the Future," 8.

6

Preaching *Invitationally*

Then Jesus said . . . , "Someone gave a great dinner and invited many. At the time for the dinner he sent his slave to say to those who had been invited, 'Come; for everything is ready now.'"

—Luke 14:16–17

The slave's invitation, "Come, for everything is ready now," has a certain liturgical resonance that echoes the traditional invitation to the eucharist: "Come, for all things are ready." The likenesses are so striking that the invitation to dinner in the parable of the host throwing a great banquet got attached to the church's weekly eucharistic meal.

The invitation was issued by the host's personal envoy. Invitations were given and responded to by word of mouth in the days before formal RSVPs. In the parable as recounted by Luke, the personal envoy issuing the invitation was the host's *doulos*, rendered in the New Revised Standard Version as "slave." Many other translations preserve the traditional "servant." To those with modern ears for hearing, "slave" conjures up images that may or may not be appropriate for the role of the *doulos* in Luke's world. "Servant" shifts the images from those of servitude to those of dutiful, willing, and loyal members of the household. Moreover, "servant" language has a long history associated generally with positive images in Judeo-Christian theology.

All of this may seem the hair-splitting of a language nerd. Yet, the shift to "servant" language focuses more attention on the *transmitter* of the invitation than on the *issuer*. Obviously the host in the story gave the instructions regarding the invitations, yet it was the servant who was sent to communicate with those whom the host had invited and to get their personal responses to the invitations. Further, "Come, for everything is ready now" viewed metaphorically, as has been the liturgical practice in the church, lifts the invitation to participation in a mystical and sacramental event.

Much has been written by denominational agencies and individual church planners and planters on "invitational preaching." "Invitational preaching" from their perspectives generally is about strategies for church growth. One such volume pictures on its cover a blue chalkboard game-plan for a football play with the movements of the offensive players, marked with O's arrowed to hit the X-marked defensive players. It's all supposed to be a "strategy" for preaching designed to win the game of church growth. This preaching scheme is just one among thousands of experience-based programs for preaching that, in essence, even if the authors are unaware, are contemporary takes on, and even perversions of, theological assumptions that harken back to those of the nineteenth-century German theologian Friedrich Schleiermacher.

The young Schleiermacher lived and moved and had his being among the literary and philosophical intelligentsia of Berlin in the late 1700s. His 1799 book *Über die Religion: Reden an die Gebildeten unter ihren Verächtern* (generally translated as *On Religion: Speeches to Its Cultured Despisers*) charted a new course for theology that even has its significant vestiges today. "Cultured Despisers" has a disdainful ring, when literally the German words mean "Well-Educated Dismissers," and "Speeches" is more formal than the style of "Conversations" that Schleiermacher employed in the book. "Religion" to his literary and artistic friends was a belief system they had dismissed as rigid and archaic. German Romanticism was budding among his well-educated literary and artistic friends, and they challenged him on his thirtieth birthday in 1778 to "write something." *Speeches*, which appeared in its first edition in 1799, was his attempt to do Christian apologetics, that is, to frame the Christian faith in a way that those who had dismissed religion, including those in his inner circle of friends, might take a second look. In an often-quoted, sometimes differently translated, passage, Schleiermacher breaks with the traditional theological thinking of the time: "Religion's essence is neither thinking (*Denken*) nor acting (*Handeln*), but intuition (*Anschauung*) and feeling (*Gefühl*). It wishes to intuit (*anschauen*) the universe, wishes devoutly to overhear the universe's own actions and manifestations, longs to be grasped and filled by the universe's immediate influences in childlike passivity."[1] Although what he meant by "universe" has been the subject of scholarly debate, it obviously means more than the physical universe of scientific research and explanation. It is more an idealistic sense of the "universal" that gets reflected in the particular, a sense of the all-in-all that is to be approached in awe and wonder. The net result was this: what Schleiermacher gave voice to in his *Speeches* invited theology—and homiletics and liturgics—into the realms of human experience.

In Schleiermacher's major work, *The Christian Faith* (*Der christliche Glaube nach den Grundsätzen der evangelischen Kirche*, 1821), he elaborated the idea that religious feeling, the sense of absolute dependence on God as communicated by Jesus through the church, is the basis for systematic theology. "The work," as one anonymous commentator puts it, "is therefore simply a description of the facts of religious feeling, or of the inner life of the soul in its relations to God, and these inward facts are looked at in the various stages of their development and presented in their systematic connection. The aim of the work was to reform Protestant theology, to put an end to the unreason and superficiality of both supernaturalism and rationalism." Schleiermacher was pushing the Reformed insistence

---

1. Friedrich Schleiermacher, *On Religion: Speeches to Its Cultured Despisers*, ed. Richard Crouter (Cambridge: Cambridge University Press, 1996), 22.

of faith or trust (total dependence on God) as the basis of theology into a new paradigm that would dominate the theological and homiletical agendas for more than a hundred years until Karl Barth and others broke the Schleiermacherian mold. Unfortunately, nearly two hundred years later there is still a great company of preachers trying to glue together faith-based, religion-based approaches to preaching, the metaphors of football strategies being one such example. The glue seems to be louder and louder amplifications of repetitive clichés accompanied by entertainment-based communication devices and increasingly sophisticated lighting and theatrical technologies.

Obviously it was not just one theologian or one book alone that gave rise to the many experience-based approaches to preaching that dominate the present homiletical landscape. Television and video personalities—some ordained, some self-proclaimed, and some media-made—appeal to a certain individualism endemic in the American experience and make millions of dollars on books, CDs, and Internet-accessible devotional guides that foster do-it-yourself religion. The religions are many, and the gods are many: religions of prosperity, personal fulfillment, lifestyle management, social engineering, self-styled spiritualities. Even public-school textbooks on American history that deal at least cursorily with the role of religion in shaping American culture narrow the religious "heroes" to the ones popularized by the media and even politics. Many students reared in totally secularized environments conclude that religion is about "that stuff," and will have nothing to do with religion. We have created multitudes of "well-educated dismissers" of religion. There is a crying need for a new Christian apologetic that invites these dismissers into the sacred mystery that lies beyond their own experience and personal needs. At the same time that he was emotionally and intellectually involved with the Berlin literary and artistic "dismissers" of religion, Schleiermacher was an ordained Reformed pastor serving the Caritas Hospital in Berlin.

A pastor in a town that previously was part of the German Democratic Republic until the Berlin Wall fell in 1989 said to me shortly thereafter: "The doorsill of the church is too high for secular people to step over by themselves." He related stories of the church's difficulties in helping people who lived under enforced secularization during the GDR to step over what seemed to them an emotional and intellectual barrier too high to step over by themselves. Although the causes of such secularization during the GDR and what has happened here in western democracies in recent decades are different, the results are strikingly similar. "Church" is foreign territory physically, emotionally, and intellectually for an increasing percentage of today's cultured dismissers of religion. And "cultured" here is not a synonym for "highly educated," but "cultured" as a product of entertainment overkill and a commercialized and media-fed culturalization in which "religion" is despised and seen as irrelevant and sometimes even depicted as demonic.

Yet, there are some who discover that the gods of culture have betrayed them and who search for more than the promises of digitalized relationship can offer them. That same German pastor told of a young man who wandered into the church the pastor was serving shortly after the fall of the Berlin Wall. Many of the church buildings date from medieval times, and a hanging crucifix is common even in churches that went through the Reformation of the sixteenth century. This young man who had obviously spent most of his life in the ideology of systematized atheism pointed to the crucifix and asked the pastor innocently and in all honesty, "Who's that guy on the cross?" There are some who want to know who's on the cross, and that knowing is not encapsulated in rational concepts and intellectual information but in a relationship with Christ that takes hold of one's life and brings resurrection and new life as present realities. There are some who want to experience relationships with other human beings that have transcendent dimensions—we call it church.

Gospeling people outside and inside the church into relationships that have both vertical and horizontal dimensions of meaning through Word and Sacrament is the church's primary task and joy in these times. Preaching *invitationally*, therefore, is very different from the kinds of *invitational* preaching that are tools for conversion and church growth. *Invitational* preaching has ulterior motives. Preaching *invitationally* is far more than the imparting of information that might bring a person to the realization that faith could change his or her life. It is that, but it is far more. Preaching *invitationally* is more than persuading. Preaching *invitationally* is the very gospeling that invites people into a mystery greater than themselves; preaching *invitationally* is enticing the assembly into the Word of God and into what God is doing *now*. In the very act of gospeling through Word and Sacrament, by the action of the Holy Spirit in a gathered assembly, the crucified and resurrected Christ *is present* in judgment and grace, himself the host inviting individuals and the gathered community, through every action of the liturgy, into the new life Christ is offering. I said in a previous chapter that preaching evangelically is inviting people into what lies between the "already" and the "not yet." It's in that in-between-ness that gospeling takes place, and it occurs intentionally, invitationally.

Gospeling invitationally, to some of us, confronts us with the first question raised by the Heidelberg Catechism more than 450 years ago yet which is still the primal question of existence: "What is your only comfort in life and in death?" and draws us into the mystery larger than a catechism's answer: "That I belong—body and soul, in life and in death—not to myself but to my faithful Savior Jesus Christ. . . ." Marva Dawn, drawing upon baptismal imagery, raises a test question for an all-inclusive approach to preaching invitationally: "What matters is that whatever songs or forms we use keep us aware that God has invited us into worship, that God is present, that God is eminently worthy to receive our praise. . . . The question is whether our worship services immerse us in God's splendor."[2] Preaching invitationally is ushering people to the edge of the great mystery that cannot be explained, and inviting the assembly to peer in and to hear the divine invitation, "Come to *me*. . . ."

2. Marva J. Dawn, *A Royal "Waste" of Time: The Splendor of Worshiping God and Being Church for the World* (Grand Rapids: Eerdmans, 1999), 158.

Inviting people into the mystery of Christ is all about gospel *hospitality*. The gospeling starts before Sunday with one-to-one invitations that arise in personal relationships and conversations throughout the week. Studies have proven that the largest percentage of visitors to churches come from personal face-to-face invitations, coupled with welcoming websites and Internet social networks that are updated weekly and responded to regularly, welcoming telephone-answering messages that are not only informational but also invitational, signage that invites and indicates where the first-time visitor can find parking and where the main entrance to the church building is.

I once wrote an article and offered a seminar for church leaders that I titled "Does Your Church Say 'Hello'?" Obviously "church" has a double meaning of both place and people. Is the church building handicapped-accessible? Are there welcomers *outside* the doors, even in the parking lot? Are there welcomers *inside* the doors assisting and directing people to coatracks, restrooms, childcare facilities? Remember, the doorsill of the church is too high even for intentional seekers. Are there those who help people to a seat and give them worship aids and even offer to sit with them?

My family and I were traveling in Puerto Rico, and I telephoned a church to find out how to get to the church. My Spanish vocabulary is limited to about a dozen words, but the person who answered the phone—it was a Sunday morning—welcomed us and gave us precise directions in English on how to find the church. When we drove up to the church, someone already was waiting for us outside and moved a car along the street so that we could find a parking place. By the way, no one knew who I was. I was simply a stranger looking for the church. Inside, a woman gave us bulletins and hymnals, offered to sit with us to help us through the Spanish liturgy, and escorted us to the communion table for the eucharist. It was an experience of outrageous gospel hospitality that I will never forget.

When passing the peace of Christ was first introduced in the liturgy in which I am the weekly presider, there was an initial hesitance on the part of some. However, within weeks, passing the peace of Christ became an act in which everyone started passing the peace to everyone else! Even two-year-olds who can't get all the words are eager to grasp hands and simply say "Peace." These minutes of peace-passing have become a noisy act of people bumping into each other to ensure that even the organist is not passed by and no one is excluded from being handed the peace of Christ. It is truly an expression of outrageous gospel hospitality and a priestly vocation in which all the baptized regardless of age can share.

This church includes the mantra of the United Church of Christ on every publication, including each Sunday's bulletin which serves as a weekly book of common prayer for the enactment of the liturgy: "Whoever you are and wherever you are on life's journey, you are welcome here." Several years ago a couple in their twenties, recent college grads and sweethearts, came to church. She had moved to the community that was his hometown. They kept coming more and more frequently. One Sunday he asked me, "What are those little envelopes people use for their offering?" I almost fell over! That was the first time in nearly fifty years of ministry that anybody ever asked for offering envelopes! It was time for a visit. I learned that she came from a religious community in the Midwest that did not practice infant baptism. He grew up in a nominally Roman Catholic family but was never baptized. They indicated their desire to receive baptism, and after some catechizing, they knelt at the font in the presence of the worshiping assembly and received baptism with water and the laying on of hands. She was ordained a year later as an elder in the congregation.

Then there is another couple—and I have received permission to share their faith-journey which they have shared publicly in worship. They are a same-sex couple who six years ago rented the church's parsonage, which is attached to the church building. They were caring for a young child who happened to be the son of one of the partners' sister. The sister was a nurse in Florida and had suffered some kind of cerebral accident that five years later continued to keep her in a coma-tose state. It was discovered at the time of the accident that she was one-month pregnant. Six months later her son was born by caesarian section, and the one partner—not the sister's sib-ling—quit her job and spent sixty days with the tiny newborn in the Florida hospital until he was strong enough to make the trip home. Initially the partners and nephew sat on the front porch on Sundays and watched those coming and going from worship. Should they venture to go up all those steps? Would they be accepted? Yes, they saw the weekly announcement: "Whoever you are and wherever you are on life's journey, you are welcome here." But would *they* be welcomed? Finally, one of them broke the ice and came to worship. Then the other partner came. Finally they both came and brought the little boy with them.

I learned much later that both had been baptized and had grown up with strong faith-roots. Before their move into the parsonage, they had attended one of the megachurches that had sprung up in the area. That church insisted on re-baptizing them, and reluctantly they were willing to submit to that mandate. The week before their scheduled rebaptism and reception, the wife of the pastor called them to a special meeting which they thought was to be a preparation for the baptism event. Instead, the pastor's wife said, "If you con-tinue in your lifestyle, you will go to hell, and you are not welcome in this church!" That's one of the reasons many SBNRs find the doorsill of the church too high to step over by themselves.

The next chapter in their faith journey began with an af-firmation of their baptism into Christ and reception into the congregation that has become home for them. Simultaneously their son was baptized, and the next day his legal adoption was finalized. Robbie said to me, "Now we are family!" A year ago the congregation elected Jennifer an elder, and she was ordained to that office in the congregation. She now is the president of the congregation. Since this state's decision—even before the Supreme Court ruling—to grant a marriage license to same-sex couples, Jennifer and Kirsten were united in holy marriage in the church—and the whole congregation was invited to the service. "Whoever you are and wherever you are on life's journey, you are welcome here" is more than a slogan. This congregation has embraced them with the gospel, invited them into the mystery of Christ, and lifted them lovingly over the church's doorsill.

7

Preaching Metaphorically

Jesus said to them, "I am the bread of life. Whoever comes to me will never be hungry, and whoever believes in me will never be thirsty."

—John 6:35

Jesus answered [Nicodemus], "Very truly, I tell you, no one can see the kingdom of God without being born from above." Nicodemus said to him, "How can anyone be born after having grown old? Can one enter a second time into the mother's womb and be born?" Jesus answered, "Very truly, I tell you, no one can enter the kingdom of God without being born of water and Spirit."

—John 3:3–5

I once had a considerable conversation with the chair of a hymnal committee over some words in traditional "memory bank" hymns such as "joy of heaven to earth come *down*," or "The heavens are not too *high* . . . the earth is not too *low*," or "Praise God, all creatures *here below*; praise him *above*, ye heavenly host" (italics mine). I was told that "we no longer live in a three-storied universe," and therefore such spatial words needed to be changed to be relevant in the modern, scientific mindset. The argument included other theological words and

concepts that need not be aired here. However, what was revealed in this conversation was an attempt, in my mind, to
"de-metaphor" some faith-affirmations and poetic expressions
that, from a metaphoric perspective, have nothing at all to do
with scientific understandings of the universe.

The word "metaphor" comes from Greek stems that mean
"to carry over" from one thing to another. Metaphors are different from similes in that they do not include the words "like"
or "as." Similes are one-to-one comparisons: The psalmist cries,
"As a deer longs for flowing streams, so my soul longs for you,
O God" (Ps. 42:1). Metaphors, on the other hand, invite a crossing over of meanings: Jesus says in John's Gospel, "I am the
bread of life" (John 6:35). Obviously, "bread" metaphorically
is not a description of what comes out of an oven. And "life"
metaphorically is not a term related to biology, that is, to the
study or knowledge of living things. Jesus, in the Gospel of
John, preaches in metaphors: "I am the light of the world"; "I
am the good shepherd"; "I am the vine, you are the branches";
"You are the salt of the earth." By the way, I learned from conversations with Gail Ramshaw—whom I consider the eminent
authority on the structure of the Revised Common Lectionary—
that the overarching theological framework of that lectionary
is essentially the Gospel of John. Gospeling, therefore, involves
allowing the rich metaphors not only of John, but also those
throughout the Bible, to immerse themselves homiletically and
liturgically in the life of assemblies. Metaphors "carry over" assemblies from what is everyday experience into mysteries and
meanings beyond the words themselves—without the necessity
to explain or provide theological and doctrinal rationales. To
hold out a broken loaf with the words, "Behold the Lamb of
God who takes away the sin of the world," invites a metaphoric
participation—in that moment—into the salvific event of Jesus
Christ crucified and risen.

Metaphors are multivalent: "death" and "life," for example,
have many layers of meaning simultaneously. "Dead" or "died"
in English translations of the Apostles' Creed are affirmations
that Jesus literally died, that is, from a biological perspective

there was no more life in his earthly body. The Creed affirms, as does the New Testament, a literal death—against what in the early church was condemned as heretical, that is, that Christ only *appeared* to have died. On the other hand, for example, when Paul writes, "So you also must consider yourselves dead to sin and alive to God in Christ Jesus" (Rom. 6:11), "dead" and "alive" are theological metaphors for the new life in Christ. In Psalm 23, "green pastures" and "still waters" are poetic metaphors "carrying over" from what was everyday experience into theological dimensions of transcendent realities. Isaac Watts convinced English-speakers that hymns can do the same thing.

Metaphors are more than symbols. Modern international traffic signage includes many symbols that previously were rendered in words: "caution," "no parking here," "one-way street." (The English "STOP" seems to have become multilingual.) A "cross" can refer to an X-shaped sign designating a place to "cross" a railway. A cross sometimes is a physical symbol placed in churches or worn as a piece of jewelry to represent the cross on which Jesus was crucified (literally "crossed" in Latin). A cross was an instrument for inflicting corporal punishment in Roman times, and it was such a brutal reminder that early Christians eschewed fashioning physical symbols of the cross. Rather, they "made" the sign of the cross as a movement of arm and hand tracing a cross on one's head and torso or simply a sign of blessing on another's forehead as in the imposition of ashes on Ash Wednesday. More will be said regarding the role of symbols in the next chapter. The present discussion continues to focus on words and word phrases as metaphors that carry over meaning from one reality to another.

When Paul writes to the Corinthian church: "The message about the cross is foolishness to those who are perishing, but to us who are being saved it is the power of God" (1 Cor. 1:18), he is preaching metaphorically. "Cross" is more than two boards nailed together to warn motorists that they are crossing railway tracks. "Cross" to Paul and the church is the very central metaphor for the power of God working for the world's salvation from the powers of sin and evil. Preaching the cross and Christ crucified metaphorically in the gathered assembly becomes, through the Holy Spirit, the very means for the "unbinding of the Gospel."[1] "Cross" as metaphor in the act of gospeling takes on sacramental dimensions of transcendent meaning. The same can be said of the metaphoric phrase, "This is my body broken for you." The "is" is more than representational language inviting historical memory. "This is my body broken for you" is a metaphor inviting participation in the sacred mystery of Christ.

An extended metaphoric form is a parable. Jesus's teaching method, which he inherited from the rabbis, frequently involved the telling of parables. Perhaps the most remembered of Jesus's teachings are the parables recorded by the synoptic Gospel writers. Parables are metaphors extended into short narratives: "Listen! A sower went out to sow . . ." (Mark 4:3). "Parable" comes from the Greek *parabolē*, "comparison," "juxtaposition," "one thing side by side to another thing." Like a metaphor, there is a crossing over of meaning in a parable: "sower" as an agricultural worker engaged in first-century farming methods crosses over *in the hearer* metaphorically as "Sower," the divine sower. The meaning is not in "sower" as a farmer ("Listen, a sower went out to sow"—Mark 4:3) but in the crossover in the hearers ("Let anyone with ears to hear listen!"—Mark 4:9). Of course, "ears," "to hear," and "listen" also are all metaphors.

That the parable of the sower found its way into all three synoptic Gospels reveals that it was preached in various settings in the church before it reached its eventual inclusion in three very similar, yet different, literary shapings. Even though it seems straightforward in its storytelling, the original form of this parable, like most of the other parables of Jesus, is difficult to discover. It had—and still has—wide appeal because it has to do with the growing of crops—essential for first-century as well as present-day societies. Of course, metaphorically it is not about farming but about the kingdom of God. In the same fourth chapter of Mark we find the reference point of the met-

1. Martha Grace Reese, *Unbinding the Gospel: Real Life Evangelism*, 2nd ed. (St. Louis: Chalice, 2008).

aphor more clearly articulated, "[Jesus] also said, 'The kingdom of God is as if someone would scatter seed on the ground . . .'" (Mark 4:26).

From today's vantage point, as Joachim Jeremias pointed out, it appears that "the sower in Mark 4:3–8 sows so clumsily that much of the seed is wasted; one might have expected a description of the regular method of sowing, and that, in fact is what we have here. This is easily understood when we remember that in Palestine sowing precedes ploughing."[2] Hence, the divine sower is not an inept farmer but, in first-century agricultural practice, knows indeed how the kingdom is sown, and the parable illustrates how changing cultural contexts bring about misunderstandings of original intentions and meanings. Jeremias goes on: "Already in the earliest period of all, during the first decade after the death of Jesus, the parables had undergone a certain amount of reinterpretation. At a very early stage the process of treating parables as allegories had begun, a process which for centuries concealed the meaning of the parables under a thick layer of dust."[3]

The tendency to interpret simple parables as allegories is found in the continuation of the parable of the sower in Mark 4:14–20, where the shift in meaning is from the sower to preaching and allegorical identifications of "good" and poor soils. Jeremias concludes, "The interpretation of the parable of the Sower misses the eschatological point of the parable. The emphasis has been transferred from the eschatological to the psychological aspect of the parable. In the interpretation the parable has become an exhortation to converts to examine themselves and test the sincerity of their conversion."[4] As the "interpretation" of the parable of the sower illustrates, preaching allegorically got a firm foothold in the church even in the second half of the first century before gos-

2. Joachim Jeremias, *The Parables of Jesus*, trans. S. H. Hooke (London: SCM, 1963), 11.
3. Jeremias, *The Parables of Jesus*, 12–13.
4. Jeremias, *The Parables of Jesus*, 78–79.

peling reached literary formats. And, unfortunately, instead of allowing the biblical metaphors and, in extended forms, parables to unleash their power in the assembly, preachers with a need to explain continue to flatten them out into didactic and moralistic "messages" about human experience instead of what God is doing.

Rodney Kennedy puts it this way: "The metaphors of the New Testament [are] disclosers of possibilities for human existence which seem and are beyond the limit of what our ordinary language and experience might imagine. I do not mean that religious metaphors present a new, supernatural world wherein we may escape the world in which we live. I do mean that metaphor *redescribes* ordinary reality in order to *disclose* a *new*, and extraordinary possibility for our lives."[5]

In a sermon for Transfiguration Sunday the biblical text was:

> Then a cloud overshadowed them, and from the cloud there came a voice, "This is my Son, the Beloved; listen to him!" As they were coming down the mountain, he ordered them to tell no one about what they had seen, until after the Son of Man had risen from the dead. (Mark 9:7–9)

The metaphor that I established in the very first sentences of the sermon was "preview," as in the "previews of coming attractions" that everyone in the assembly had experienced in movie theaters. The sermon began:

> When Ruth and I go to the movies—which is rarely—we try to time our arrival in the theater so that we walk in just about at the end of the previews. We really don't want to pay for a bombardment of gunfire and explosions in films that will come to the theater up to half a year to nine months in advance. We try to skip the previews of coming *distractions*.

5. Rodney Kennedy, *The Creative Power of Metaphor: A Rhetorical Homiletic* (Lanham, MD: University Press of America, 1993), 75.

Immediately the scene shifted to Mt. Tabor in Israel, identified traditionally as the mountain of transfiguration:

> Each year on the Sunday before Ash Wednesday we are presented the story of Jesus's transfiguration. The Gospel story—it's almost identical in Matthew and Mark—is this account of Jesus taking Peter, James, and John on a hike up Mt. Tabor. Mark tells us it was "a high mountain." Actually Mt. Tabor is geologically a monadnock, a kind of overgrown hill that looks like a volcano but isn't. Mt. Tabor, or *Har Tavor* in Hebrew, pokes itself up from the Galilean plain. Across the centuries Mt. Tabor became a shrine for religious pilgrimages, and today there's a paved road so that small busses can take tourists to the top. There the Franciscans built a shrine about a hundred years ago. It's called the "Church of the Transfiguration." By the way, Mt. Tabor has been developed as one of Israel's premier locales for hang-gliders to jump off and sail back down into the valley below!

The metaphor, "preview," had been introduced, the setting both of the transfiguration story and as a place of tourism today, had been identified, and then the narrative began:

> Mark says, "Jesus took with him Peter and James and John, and led them up a high mountain apart, by themselves. And he was transfigured before them, and his clothes became dazzling white, such as no one on earth could bleach them." Transfiguration is a changing of form—in this case from whatever attire Jesus was wearing for the hike to clothes more dazzling white than even Clorox could bleach.
>
> And to add to the drama, two of Israel's heroes long dead appear—Moses and Elijah, and they start up a conversation with Jesus. Peter, who always was the most impulsive of the disciples, blurted out—even though he and the other two were absolutely terrified—Peter suggested making three shrines there on Mt. Tabor—one for Jesus, one for Moses, one for Elijah. But immediately the mountain was shrouded

in a cloud, and from the cloud a voice: "This is my Son, the Beloved. Listen to him." And when Peter and James and John looked around, there was no one there but Jesus in his regular hiking clothes. Incredible!

This is simply a narration of the Gospel story. Yet, the last word was "Incredible!" the intention of which was to signal, without explanation, that there was a mystery in the making.

Then the sermon shifted to the hearers and began to raise what I call the "So what?" homiletical questions:

This is one of the stories that Thomas Jefferson literally scissored out of his Bible. This is one of the kinds of Bible stories that convince unbelievers of the validity of their atheism. This is one of *those* stories that just goes too far for the spiritual-but-not-religious to embrace. It stretches the rubber bands of religion just too far. Instantly Cloroxed clothes are a scientific impossibility. Dead men in conversation with Jesus is an affront to rational thinking. The mount of transfiguration is too high for secular people even to approach, moreover even to start the hike.

So why build shrines, even just one shrine there on top of this geological monadnock? Even Jesus nixed Peter's plans. Why even repeat and reread this story that seems so fantastic and unbelievable? By the way, the voice from heaven on Mt. Tabor speaks the same words that came from heaven at Jesus's baptism in the Jordan: "This is my Son, the Beloved." We encounter the same words at the beginning of Epiphany with Jesus's baptism and again at the end of Epiphany on the Mount of Transfiguration before the plunge down into the depths of Lent.

Any attempt to explain homiletically what Mark narrates would be foolhardy, although I know some preachers have tried. Instead I tried to let the mystery be a mystery and invite the assembly into it.

The "why?" of all of this—and remember, the Bible wants to ask the "why" questions before the "how" questions—the "why" of the transfiguration story is revealed in the trek down the mountain. By the way, they didn't hang-glide down from the top, but took the pathway down! And, along that pathway, Jesus, according to Mark, "ordered them to tell no one about what they had seen, until after the Son of Man had risen from the dead." There's the clue to the "why" of Transfiguration. Now, normal people who have seen an epiphany of Cloroxed clothes and dead men speaking aren't going to keep quiet about it. Normal people wouldn't keep such theophanies secret. But the Bible isn't about normal things. Mark says Jesus ordered them to keep this all a secret until after he himself is raised from the dead.

In other words, the whole epiphany on Mt. Tabor, the whole episode of transfiguration, according to Mark, was an intended *preview* of the resurrection, a *preview* of Easter. *Then*, they could remember Mt. Tabor's epiphany, *then* they could see the intention of this mountaintop experience. Transfiguration is the *preview* of resurrection.

Jesus's prohibition on the hike down the mountain made no sense to his companions—until *after* resurrection and they could be brought by the risen Christ to the remembrance of the epiphany: "Aha! Now we know, now it is clear that our time on the mountain was a preview of what resurrection is. Now we have a foretaste of being with Jesus and all the saints in glory." They were clueless on the hike down the mountain, but it all began to be revealed after "He is risen!" was shouted by the women on Easter's morning. And so, every year on the last Sunday of Epiphany, the Sunday before Ash Wednesday, we are confronted by the Transfiguration story to give us a preview of what will happen *after* Good Friday, *after* the crucifixion, *after* the cross, *after* the burial. The Transfiguration is a preview of Easter.

The metaphor "preview" crossed over from that which is commonly experienced in movie theaters to an open-ended theological question, the answer to which can be given from a scholarly perspective—which would not be homiletically appropriate—or the raising of an existential question that carries over those gathered into questions not only of Jesus's resurrection, but of their own future with God. The metaphor pushes itself multivalently into other dimensions of the Christian life both in this world here and now and eschatologically in what is yet to come, individually and corporately as the church.

Let's jump back to Peter's architectural plans to build three shrines. There's something in Peter and in most human beings that wants to linger in moments of spiritual ecstasy. Peter wanted to enshrine the moment. But then, what is a reality beyond human making would become a thing, a granite memorial to a past encounter, rather than a foretaste of what is yet to happen. There's something that's part of our humanness that wants to enshrine past glories instead of anticipating the glory that is yet to be revealed—in this life and in the world to come. God only gives the preview of what is to come and then the cloud disappears, and it is as if God says, "For now, folks, that's all. Go down the mountain in remembrance of the preview, but look to the real epiphany that is yet to happen." The church, brothers and sisters, lives in the remembrance of the preview, in the lingering light of the preview of glory but in expectation of being changed from glory into glory—in the life to come, but changed in this life also.

Human beings are terribly forgetful of their glimpses of glory. Even those closest to Jesus in the flesh were forgetful. On that fateful Friday when their Savior hung dying as a criminal, there's no report of their having remembered the preview on Mt. Tabor. Even on Easter, even on the day when what had been previewed happened, Scripture is silent about their remembering the preview on the mount of transfiguration. When bad things happen, there's a certain amnesia of the preview that sets in for us human beings. Funerals have a way of becoming only ways of remembering the past rather than being a preview of what is to come. In African American Christian cultures, a funeral is a "going home" service. Rather than just a remembering of things past, a funeral is really a preview of going home, not only a going home of the one who died, but also a preview of our own going home. We humans—even those closest to Jesus in the flesh—have a way of forgetting or even blocking out the preview of Easter, even our own Easter.

Yet, ever since Mary realized that the one she thought was the gardener was her crucified and risen Lord, every Lord's Day, every Sunday, is the preview. Every Sunday that we hear the gospel proclaimed, we are reminded that this is the preview of being home. Every time we break bread, we are reminded that each communion is the preview of heaven's banquet. Every Sunday we come to church for the preview of home. Every Sunday, Jesus brings to us the remembrance that right here, right now we are in the very midst of the preview.

The ending of a sermon—I purposely do not say "conclusion"—is an integral part of the "carry over." This is not a time for summing up and repeating the "points," as in a lecture, to make sure everybody "gets it" intellectually. Rather, a sermon is only one part of a total engagement with the Word of God, and it will transition itself into what will yet happen liturgically following the sermon. The end of the homiletical event leads into other liturgical events—including baptism and eucharist—that are part of the total encounter with the word of God. Sometimes a sermon's ending is shaped as a kind of homiletical interlude into what will follow.

I suggest that an alternative, as in the following ending of the Transfiguration sermon, the final words pile metaphorically upon one another, and the sermon hangs in abrupt silence, like a musical rest, in which the sounds of the last note reverberate throughout the room. This allows those with ears who have been hearing the words, to listen in silence for the Word of God and to let the Word reverberate in multiple levels of meaning. The Transfiguration Sunday sermon ends in this way:

> Peter and James and John had the luxury of a preview of heaven, yet they were ordered not to tell anyone until after Jesus's resurrection. And then, at the tomb where the women had come to mourn, the angel of God commanded instead: "Go, tell his disciples and Peter that he has been raised from the dead and will go before you into Galilee where you will see him." And they went, and they told, and others went and told, and we are here today because others went and told—what the preview promised. And the angel continues, "Go and tell." "Go and invite others to the preview, each week, come and see, come and hear, come and taste, come and experience the perpetual preview, the weekly preview that promises eternity."

Preaching metaphorically invites the assembly into experiencing multiple levels of meaning. Gail Ramshaw, referring to the whole liturgical event, including the sermon, says, "Christian liturgy is the communal celebration of biblical metaphors."[6] The many metaphors of the Gospel of John, for example, are invitations into multivalent realities. The story of Jesus and Nicodemus is a classic one, capturing the multivalent dimensions of the Greek adverb *anōthen.* Jesus, according to John's gospeling, says to Nicodemus, "Very truly, I tell you, no one can see the kingdom of God without being born *anōthen*" (John 3:3). Nicodemus was a learned leader, and according to John's account, he took the adverb to mean, in its nonmetaphoric sense, "again." "How can anyone be born after having grown old? Can one enter a second time into the mother's womb and be born?" he asks. The verb "born" (*gennēthē*) and the Greek adverb, *anōthen*, are metaphors inviting meaning beyond the everyday "born" as a biological process and "again" as "a second time."

6. Gail Ramshaw, *God Beyond Gender: Feminist Christian God-Language* (Minneapolis: Augsburg, 1995), 114.

At another level, *anōthen*, as translated into English in some versions of the New Testament, can also mean "from above," and the New Revised Standard Version renders Jesus's response to Nicodemus's supposed misunderstanding as "Do not be astonished that I said to you, 'You must be born from above.'" Jesus, according to John, expands the "from above" metaphor to refer to "of water and Spirit," images of baptism. And "Spirit," too, is multivalent in Greek and Hebrew. "Wind" and "Spirit" are the same word, and so in this encounter between Jesus and Nicodemus, there emerges another metaphor, "wind"/"Spirit." John is gospeling metaphorically and inviting preachers to preach metaphorically and assemblies to hear metaphorically. The question to Nicodemus, "Are you a teacher of Israel, and yet you do not understand these things?" is intended homiletically for more than just one hearer with ears to hear.

The conversation between Jesus and Nicodemus in this Gospel story exemplifies so much in contemporary social, political, and religious discourse. Nicodemus simply "didn't get it," and in the aftermath of the Enlightenment in western cultures in the seventeenth and eighteenth centuries, most of those schooled in rationalism and secularism "don't get it" either. Meaning is reduced, in the words of Gail Ramshaw, to the "flattened babble of email."[7] Communication is degraded into misspelled text messages and Twitter "tweets," and the complications of world events are relegated to three-sentence reports by TV newscasters. (Count the sentences sometime in the evening news!) Biblical literalists, ironically, employ the same rationalistic hermeneutical constructs they condemn. Religious fundamentalists of every stripe and political ideology take license to reduce sacred texts into brutal instruments of indoctrination and even torture. Three-point sermons designed to explain biblical "truths" as proverbs for the development of personal piety fall short of gospeling the mystery of Christ. Overall, the world is supersaturated by informational overkill

7. Gail Ramshaw, *Liturgical Language: Keeping It Metaphoric, Making It Inclusive* (Collegeville, MN: Liturgical Press, 1996), 12.

and starved of the means of grace. We are not saved by more information! I recently saw a newsstand paperback supposedly containing a thousand *facts* (italics mine) in the Bible! Since when has the record of God's love affair with the creation been reduced to a thousand *facts*?

There was a time in public education when the curricula included the memorization and recitation of poetry (including learning how to sing and read music). However, when the teaching of science and math (and sports!) became primary, poetry and music were deemed less essential and sometimes have been dropped from academic agendas. What poetry and music teach, however, is the ability to think metaphorically, therefore imaginatively. Young children, before logic overrules imagination, are able to relate to reality metaphorically better than most adults. Luke gospels Jesus: "Truly I tell you, whoever does not receive the kingdom of God as a little child will never enter it" (Luke 18:17). "Kingdom of God," of course, is metaphoric language, and the implication is that children's perception of metaphoric realities is a spiritual discipline needed to be cultivated by adult disciples.

The following prayer of confession was crafted as a transposition of the following text from the letter to the Ephesians:

> Let no evil talk come out of your mouths, but only what is useful for building up, as there is need, so that your words may give grace to those who hear. (Eph. 4:29)

Note the metaphors and the juxtaposition of "Word" and "words":

> O God, whose Word was in the beginning of creation
>   and became flesh in Jesus Christ:
> We confess that sometimes we are careless with human
>   words—
>   words that are spoken quickly,
>   yet have such lasting effects,
>   words that spill easily in anger from our lips,

yet wound deeply those on whom they fall,
words that wear pleasant outward faces
    yet disguise less than benign inward intents,
words that come cheaply in anonymity,
    yet cost dearly in human intimacy,
words that promise faithfully in adversity,
    yet forget unconsciously in prosperity.
O God whose Word is both judgment and grace,
    tell us the ways our words can hurt,
        but speak to us also the saving Word that heals.
    Amen.[8]
    [*silence*]

The purpose of any prayer of confession is to acknowledge the theological and ethical disjuncture between God and us: our words are not God's Word, our ways are not God's ways. "Word" is a theological metaphor that confronts our flattened, email-like words, with judgment and grace. Something of the human dilemma is verbalized in the prayer of confession through the comparisons of "quickly"/"lasting," "spill easily"/"wound deeply," "come cheaply"/"cost dearly," "promise faithfully"/"forget unconsciously." Obviously words in a strictly descriptive sense do not "wear pleasant outward faces," yet the metaphor crosses meaning over so that we can say, "Yes, words *do* indeed sometimes 'wear pleasant outward faces, yet disguise less-than-benign inward intents,'" for we all *have experienced* the painful consequences of what those pleasant-faced words conceal. This is our confession to God and to one another.

The Rev. Dr. Martin Luther King Jr. was a master of metaphor. Consider the wonderful metaphors in but two snippets from his famous 1963 "I Have a Dream" address on the steps of the Lincoln memorial in Washington—an address that to me is more of a sermon than a speech: "Now is the time to rise from

---

8. F. Russell Mitman, *Worship in the Shape of Scripture*, 2nd ed. (Cleveland: Pilgrim, 2009), 83–84.

the desolate valley of segregation to the sunlit path of racial justice." Or, "The sweltering summer of the Negro's legitimate discontent will not pass until there is an invigorating autumn of freedom and equality." He was preaching metaphorically, and the power of his metaphors invited a nation into the promise of a new reality.

8

Preaching *Multisensorily*

Let my prayer be counted as incense before you, and the lifting up of my hands as an evening sacrifice.
—Psalm 141:1–2

And wherever [Jesus] went, into villages or cities or farms, they laid the sick in the marketplaces, and begged him that they might touch even the fringe of his cloak; and all who touched it were healed.
—Mark 6:56

O taste and see that the LORD is good; happy are those who take refuge in him.
—Psalm 34:8

She said to the people, "Come and see a man who told me everything I have ever done! He cannot be the Messiah, can he?"
—John 4:28–29

In my original outline for these reflections on the homiletical and liturgical arts, I titled this chapter, "Preaching Nonverbally." Yet, as this discussion began to take shape, it became clear to me not only that "nonverbal" can be construed negatively but also that what I intend to be about is more than just an absence of words. "Multisensorily" includes any or all of the five senses, and all five senses are receptors for the gospel

Word that is indeed verbal but also involves more than words. Preaching multisensorily includes gospeling visually, tastably, olfactorily, and tactually, as well as auditorily. The latter has ascended to primary status in post-Enlightenment Protestantism and in literate cultures dependent on words. Yet, the church, from its infancy, has employed all five senses in the preaching of the gospel, modes that harken back to Jewish and other pre-Christian religious practices.

I have known Michael for more than forty years. When he was a teenager, his parents hoped that he could receive the rite of confirmation. In those days confirmation instruction was essentially catechetical and involved rational instruction in Bible and church doctrine. Michael was born with Down syndrome, and the traditional approach, I believed, would not work. Instead I engaged with Michael in a one-to-one mentoring program that centered on multisensory physical symbols, liturgical actions, and body movements of prayer and rites and sacraments. Michael received the confirmation of his baptism, and thirty years later at a dinner recognizing my retirement Michael was there and testified publicly and excitedly, "He did this" (as he made the sign of the cross on his forehead) "to me!"

Michael's testimony reflected powerfully a saying attributed to St. Francis of Assisi: "Preach the gospel; use words if necessary." Michael taught me that preaching is not restricted to the words of a homily or sermon. The whole liturgy preaches. All the actions proclaim. Words are attached to most of what happens when an assembly gathers, yet, preaching occurs multisensorily as well. The eucharist, for example, gospels the holy mystery through all five senses: *auditorily* through the spoken words of institution, eucharistic prayer, and administration; *visually* through the breaking of the bread and the pouring of the cup; *tactually* through receiving the bread in the hand and handling the cup; *tastably* through eating bread and drinking wine; and even *olfactorily* through smelling fresh-baked bread (not wafers!) and the aroma of hearty wine. Christ is proclaimed, offered, and received through all five senses in one act.

When I was a child, holy communion was celebrated only

four times a year in the church of which my family was part. One of those celebrations was on Easter. My father was an elder, and one of the responsibilities associated with that office was the preparation of the communion elements, which generally occurred on Holy Saturday. It was a big deal to cut up with the precision of a surgeon several hundred cubes of bread and to fill tiny individual glasses of wine by means of a silver device with a rubber bulb that squirted precisely one individual glass-full of wine. (I never tasted grape juice in communion until I went to college!) I theorize that perhaps one of the reasons for infrequent communion is that preparation and cleanup of all the dishes is such a major undertaking! The elders carried all of these trays of bread and wine into the church's chancel, placed them on the altar table, and covered them with a white linen cloth. I was obliged to go to the church with my father and to watch all these preparations. Of course, come Easter Sunday I was not "allowed" to eat the bread and drink the wine because I had not yet received the "license" through the rite of confirmation. Yet, what I remember from those Holy Saturday preparations was the enticing aroma of wine emanating from those hundreds of individual glasses. I can still smell the wine—which, by the way, was offered by the proprietress of one of the town's pubs. The whole church smelled holy, and I could smell Easter coming!

The use of incense goes back to ancient cultic practices in the Near East. The burning of incense was a priestly function in Jewish temple worship, prescribed elaborately in the Torah and linked to sacrificial practices. In Psalm 141:2 it is a metaphor for prayer: "Let my prayer be counted as incense before you." In Matthew's narrative of the Epiphany the gifts offered by the magi included "frankincense and myrrh," two varieties of incense associated with anointing of royalty and an offering fit for a deity. In the apocalyptic language of the book of Revelation, an "angel with a golden censer came and stood at the altar; he was given a great quantity of incense to offer with the prayers of all the saints on the golden altar that is before the throne. And the smoke of the incense, with the prayers of the saints, rose before God from the hand of the angel" (Rev. 8:3–5). Despite condemnation of the use of incense by some Hebrew prophets—particularly Second Isaiah, Hosea, and Ezekiel—and its exclusion from early Christian worship because of its association with pagan practices, there has been an interesting history of the use and non-use of incense that sometimes was the result of nonliturgical issues and arguments.

Today, incense still is considered "too Catholic" for many Protestant noses, although in the secular world the marketing of incense and aromas for pleasure and therapeutic purposes is at an all-time high, ironically, even among the theologically apposed. Churches in the eastern part of the Roman Empire, now mainly those in the Orthodox tradition, were quick to adopt the use of incense in the Divine Liturgy. And I wonder what difference there is in the olfactory lobes of people who each Sunday are bathed in the sweet smells of incense and those who are ready to make an appointment with their allergist after a mere whiff of the holy!

The visual and olfactory experiences of seeing and smelling burning incense are powerful multisensory acts inviting the assembly into a corporate immersion in sacred realities. The multiple layers of meaning surrounding the metaphor proclaim, that is, literally, gospel (as a verb) people into the very mystery of Christ. The actions of censing the gospel book, the reader, and the hearers are powerful signs that the Word is more than words and that through the reading from the holy book and the preaching of the Word, the Holy Spirit is gospeling this gathered assembly into a holy happening. And the beauty of incense is that it lingers olfactorily long after the benediction is given and candles are extinguished and the last worshiper goes through the door. It may be that the power of this olfactory experience is one of the reasons the burning of incense has been both embraced and abhorred throughout the Christian world for nearly two thousand years. It may take that long again for some of the faithful to accept a thurifer swinging a thurible, with its emitted billows of sanctifying smoke!

Yet, children now are ready to be awed in an Epiphany assembly with the igniting of frankincense while the gospel story of the arrival of the magi is read and the smoke arising from the burning pot of incense continues through the sermon. Or, as preface to prayer in a service of evening prayer:

A pot of burning incense may be brought to the place where prayers will be offered.

Leader: Let my prayer be counted as incense before you,
All: **and the lifting up of my hands**
                as an evening sacrifice.   —Psalm 141:2

All may lift up hands as the leader prays:

Leader: We lift up our hands to you, O God,
           and we offer all that has been part of this day to you:
           the good and the bad,
           the fulfilling and the frustrating,
           the times we have honored you and affirmed others,
           the times we have disobeyed you and harmed others.
           To you we lift up
           all we have thought and said and done,
           asking you to forgive us
           when we have missed the mark
           of your intentions for us,
           and to bless us when, in our finite and human ways,
           we have accomplished
           what you have wanted us to do.
           Through Jesus Christ, our Lord.
All: **Amen.**[1]

I have introduced incense in three congregations, and both they and I have survived the holy smoke! Assemblies may not

---

1. F. Russell Mitman, "A Liturgy for Evening Prayer," in *Blessed by the Presence of God: Resources for Occasional Services* (Cleveland: Pilgrim, 2007), 43.

accept the idea of burning incense as they remember or perceive how it takes place in other churches, yet when it happens to them in a new and different setting accompanied by words of Scripture and prayer, censing can become a means of preaching multisensorily and of engaging assemblies in realities beyond ordinary sense experience.

Baptism is the sacrament of God's grace that from a human perspective is proclaimed and received multisensorily. Depending on the tradition, there are always words spoken and heard auditorily. There is water, the amount of which varies from tradition to tradition, from a candy-dish-full to a bathtub-full to a whole river-full or even ocean-full. We see the sacramental water being administered—by sprinkling, pouring, or immersion *visually*. The one being baptized—regardless of age—certainly experiences the water *tactually*. I learned from the ancient *Didache* ("If you do not have fresh water, then use warm water") that warm water as a sacramental bath is better received tactually as a sign act of God's warm embrace than a cold shower—by both babies and adults! Baptism in most Christian traditions is the one-time sacrament. Yet, there are many opportunities to experience tactually drops of water being sprinkled in the rite of asperges—not only when another person is baptized but also when the biblical texts refer to baptism. It is the touch of the drops of water or the dipping of fingers into the font that provide for repeated tactile moments of baptismal remembrance. See chapter 3.

Baptism is the one-time sacrament of initiation into the body of Christ, and grace is infused for a lifetime. Yet, it is joined with the repeated sacrament of holy communion as a meal of spiritual nourishment in the body of Christ. And it is assumed in practice—at least by this commentator—that the bath will be followed liturgically by the meal and that both bath and meal will be joined homiletically with the Word read and preached. When all acts are joined together Christ is gospeled and received multisensorily through all of the five receptors God has created in those gathered in assembly for Word and Sacrament.

The account of the risen Christ coming to the apostle Thomas, in John's Gospel, is itself an example of preaching multisensorily. John is not interested in sharing biographical information about Jesus in the flesh as much as in proclaiming Christ crucified and risen. The Gospel of John homiletically invites those with ears to hear into an encounter with the Easter Christ and the new life that is possible for those who are in Christ. In the after-Easter account of the apostles' preaching the resurrection, in which Christ himself is present, Thomas was absent in the first encounter. The disciples gathered on that occasion told—that is, preached to—Thomas: "We have seen the Lord" (John 20:25), the same proclamation they had received from Mary Magdalene. "See" in John's Gospel is a multivalent metaphor that is meant to be more than an ophthalmic perception. But Thomas is portrayed by John as construing "seeing" visually, and responds, "Unless I see the mark of the nails in his hands, and put my finger in the mark of the nails and my hand in his side, I will not believe" (John 20:15). A week later, according to John, the risen Christ appears again and invites Thomas: "Put your finger here and see my hands. Reach out your hand and put it in my side" (John 20:27). Note the multivalent and multisensory dimensions John intends with "see" and "put your finger" ("touch"). John is evangelically inviting the assembly to "see" and "touch" homiletically and liturgically the presence of the risen One in order that, as John says in the conclusion, they may respond with Thomas, "My Lord and my God," and "may come to believe that Jesus is the Messiah, the Son of God, and that through believing you may have life in his name" (John 20:31). Preaching today on this text provides the assembly with the opportunity multivalently and multisensorily "to hear," "to see," "to touch" realities beyond themselves. Or, in the words of Horatius Bonar's eucharistic hymn:

> Here, O our Lord, we see you face to face.
> Here would we touch and handle things unseen;
> here grasp with firmer hand eternal grace,
> and all our weariness upon you lean.

Here would we feed upon the bread of God,
here drink with you the royal wine (cup) of heaven;
here would we lay aside each earthly load,
and taste afresh the calm of sin forgiven.

This is the hour of banquet and of song;
this is the heavenly table for us spread.
Here let us feast and feasting, still prolong
the eucharist of living wine and bread.[2]

The hymn captures in a prayer to Christ—and when verbalized through corporate singing, preaches Christ—in wonderful multisensory metaphors of what eucharist is: seeing, touching, handling, grasping, leaning, feeding, drinking, laying aside, tasting.

Preaching tactually engages the sense of touch. Much of worship—particularly in Protestant pews—is most often out of touch. Assemblies most often are touch-deprived. Kimberly Long in her wonderful treatise for worship leaders, *The Worshiping Body: The Art of Leading Worship*, includes a full chapter titled "The Hands: Gesture and Touch." She comments:

It must be acknowledged that in North American culture people have difficulty thinking of touch in non-sexual terms. Myriad cases of clergy sexual misconduct have raised our awareness—and our indignation—at the abuses that have been perpetrated on others. Yet we would be poorer as a community if we allowed the abuses of some to rob the rest of us of an inherently human part of worship. In services of baptism and confirmation, ordination and commissioning, healing and wholeness, to name just a few instances, touch is a crucial part of how we enact a living faith. Even as simple a gesture as sharing the peace of Christ involves the clasping of hands or embracing of one another. In fact, it is the gesture here: whether we get along with each other or not—

2. Horatius Bonar, 1855, alt.

whether we even know each other—we express our unity and our common prayer for Christ's peace through touch.[3]

It became apparent to me many years ago that there are some who gather for worship who have not been touched by another human during the week since the assembly last assembled. The depersonalizing of relationships through electronic media and the scattering of families across vast miles from each other have created touch-deprived people and, therefore, touch-deprived assemblies. The swiping of a credit card has replaced handing cash to the grocery-store checker, and thereby receiving some change in the hand in return. There are some people who do not want to be touched either because of some psychological aversion or fear of transmitting disease. I have quipped that in a culture that wants to be so sanitary maybe we need to pass out surgical gloves before the passing of the peace!

Kimberly Long continues:

As eloquent as our words may be, it is the sensation of touch that communicates beyond words when we lay on hands and pray for the empowering Spirit, or for healing. For in that touch we enact the bond with one another which we have in Jesus Christ through our baptism; we convey that no one of us goes through challenges or hardship alone; we act out, with our own bodies, the incarnational faith that we share. The transcendent God, who is so far beyond us, draws near to us through touch.[4]

Traditionally the passing of the peace occurs in the eucharist, immediately before communing, to fulfill Jesus's commandment in Matthew, "first be reconciled to your brother or sister, and then come and offer your gift" (Matt. 5:25). That is the human dimension of reconciliation; yet there is also the divine dimension—

3. Kimberly Bracken Long, *The Worshiping Body: The Art of Leading Worship* (Louisville: Westminster John Knox, 2009), 88.

4. Long, *The Worshiping Body*, 89.

the gift of forgiveness of sin and the reconciliation with God and one another that we experience in the act of confessing sin publicly and receiving the promise of forgiveness liturgically. The passing of the peace as a response to confession and forgiveness takes on sacramental dimensions: literally passing Christ to the neighbor who also has received reconciliation and forgiveness. I have interpreted the act in the congregation I serve: "In this act you are proclaiming the reconciling love of Christ and in your priestly vocation sacramentally passing Christ to each other." Touching is preaching—multisensorily. What has become so amazing in this assembly is that no one is left out in the passing of the peace. Everyone gives to everyone, and everyone receives from everyone—even the tiniest of babies. Sometimes it is also an embrace, sometimes even a kiss—the kiss of Christ. The kiss of peace is neither sentimental nor sexual; it is sacramental.

More than forty years ago, a physician who also was an elder in the church I was serving one day said to me, "Russ, I think we need to consider services of laying on of hands for spiritual healing." I gulped and responded that I would look into it. There did not seem to be much help available, either theologically or liturgically. And to those of us trained in existential philosophy and theology there was not much room for what TV evangelists were promoting as spiritual healing, often in opposition to medicine and other traditional healing arts. But, since the request came from a physician and a good friend, I had to do some research. Fortunately at about the same time I had the privilege to attend a weeklong institute in which the featured presenter was Dr. Morton Kelsey, Episcopal priest, counselor, and lecturer on the history and practice of healing in the church. His teaching, followed by the physician's and my reading of Kelsey's *Healing and Christianity*,[5] led to the creation of a service of anointing and laying on of hands for healing that became part of the Sunday service of Word and Sacrament monthly. Most often those who came and knelt at

5. Morton T. Kelsey, *Healing and Christianity* (New York: Harper & Row, 1976).

the chancel steps for the anointing and laying on of hands did
so in intercession for others. I remember distinctly when one
man who owned a nationwide trucking firm and who had a
corporate jet and private pilot so that he could manage his
various depots throughout the country knelt down one day and
said, "I come for the young man who washes my trucks. He was
just diagnosed with lymphoma." Kelsey said at the conclusion
of his exhaustive study of the church's healing ministry from
its biblical foundations to today's recovery of it:

> Today's unilateral understanding of reality is inadequate,
> and . . . a less partial view of the world is needed . . . a firm
> belief that there is some other-than-material reality which
> can make a creative change in the souls and minds and bod-
> ies of [humans]. In Christian terminology, the first require-
> ment is for a theology in which the Spirit with the gift of
> healing has an essential place. If this is accomplished before
> anything else, then the healing ministry becomes a natural
> part of our religious activity and function.[6]

I discovered that when the act of anointing and laying on of
hands became an integrated and regular part of a service of
Word and Sacrament, indeed it did become a natural compo-
nent of worship. Secondly, although I had affirmed the church's
mandate in Jesus's name to preach and teach, I purposely had
demythologized "to heal" and failed to realize that to heal is to
preach Christ, that is, to gospel the good news of the kingdom
of God of which healing is a sign. I am eternally grateful for
the impetus that Dr. Bob gave not only for the praxis of healing
services in the church but for enticing me to realize that my
God was too small.

I subsequently updated and published the liturgy for
anointing and laying on of hands[7] first prompted by the

---

6. Kelsey, *Healing and Christianity*, 345, 348.
7. F. Russell Mitman, "Anointing for Healing," in *Blessed by the Presence
of God.*

physician-elder in that church. And I have carefully introduced
the theology and praxis of this act in two other churches and in
some assemblies of the wider church. I am continually amazed
by assemblies' interest in integrating services for healing in
their ministries and, after a while, the understanding that the
praxis is simply doing what Jesus sent out ordinary people to
do as he did: preach, teach, and heal. The liturgy that is used
month after month always includes the reading of a portion of
the Epistle of James:

Leader: A reading from the Letter of James.
           Listen for the Word of God.

           Are any among you suffering? They should pray. Are any
           cheerful? They should sing songs of praise. Are any among
           you sick? They should call for the elders of the church and
           have them pray over them, anointing them with oil in the
           name of the Lord. The prayer of faith will save the sick, and
           the Lord will raise them up; and anyone who has committed
           sins will be forgiven. Therefore confess your sins to one an-
           other, and pray for one another, so that you may be healed.
           The prayer of the righteous is powerful and effective. (James
           5:14–16)

Leader: The Word of God for the people of God.
All: **Thanks be to God.**

I am amazed by the participation of children receiving anointing and laying on of hands for their friends and relatives. It is
now considered the "normal" thing for the church to do.

Foot-washing and/or hand-washing are tactile acts of
preaching multisensorily. Washing is traditionally part of the
Maundy Thursday liturgy. Yet, washing also is a powerful act
communicating and receiving forgiveness on other occasions
as well. It is not only the experience of immersing hands or
feet in the water and feeling the cleansing water, but also the
drying of feet or hands by those officiating is a means, with or

without words, of preaching and receiving the gospel tactually. In the Maundy Thursday gospel reading, John records Jesus as saying, "So if I, your Lord and Teacher, have washed your feet, you also ought to wash one another's feet. For I have set you an example, that you also should do as I have done to you" (John 13:14–15). Being touched by human hands drying one's hands or feet with a towel is a way of receiving the gospel tactually, and the one doing the drying is engaged in an act of preaching the gospel. At this writing, Maundy Thursday's liturgy is now a week past, yet what lingers is the sensation of the cleansing water and Julianna's toweling my hands dry. Liturgical washing is not a private act; it requires the "other" to fulfill Christ's priest-ing command.

A book by Greek Orthodox priest Fr. Andreas Andreopoulos, *The Sign of the Cross: The Gesture, the Mystery, the History*, opened me theologically and spiritually to an ancient gesture that was foreign to this sensorily deprived Protestant. In the chapter "Experiencing the Sign of the Cross," he says:

> What is so fascinating about the sign of the cross: its simplicity. A cross is how illiterate people sign a document because it is the simplest recognizable sign they can draw. . . . And though the cross is perhaps one of the simplest things in Christian ritual, it clearly connects with some of the greatest Christian mysteries. . . . The most profound and incomprehensible mysteries are connected with such simple objects or symbols, which somehow manage to evoke them immediately, at an impulse, a gesture. . . . Perhaps the symbol that combines simplicity and profound meaning to a greater extent than any other symbol is the sign of the cross.[8]

Now I get a glimpse into why that sign of the cross I made on Michael's forehead forty years ago left on him such an indelible impression.

---

8. Andreas Andreopoulos, *The Sign of the Cross: The Gesture, the Mystery, the History* (Brewster, MA: Paraclete, 2006), 8–9.

I also have discovered for myself that the physical movement of tracing the cross on my body, from head to each shoulder, is a tactile way of contemplative prayer that I had not experienced earlier in my life—with or without words. "The sign of the cross as wordless prayer,"[9] simply tracing the sign of the cross, to us overly verbal westerners, can lead to a significant spiritual discovery. With words, I join the signing with the ancient Jesus prayer: "Jesus Christ, Son of God, have mercy on me, a sinner," and then move into an intercessory mode: "Jesus Christ, Son of God, have mercy on _____." Fr. Andreopoulos writes: "The origins of the sign of the cross are lost in the unwritten tradition of the church. Our information is sparse because this ancient practice emerged naturally as something that made sense to most Christians."[10] The idea of making a sign on the forehead was a practice chronicled in the Old Testament. To early Christians, "the sign of the cross was a blessing so necessary to them in a time when the world was turning upside down. . . . In this chaotic time, Christians chose to bless themselves with the sign of Christ. The few witnesses to this from the early church suggest how immediately widespread this gesture must have been."[11]

Yet, there is also, and primarily, a corporate dimension to the sign of the cross. The sign is placed on the forehead in baptism and liturgically in many acts of blessing—the water, the bread, the wine, the oil in chrism. These were and still are practices that must not be seen as acts of magic or of satanic cults. Rather, the acts are accompanied with epicletic prayers that the blessing may be effected by God through the Holy Spirit and in the presence of an assembly of two or three or more gathered in the name of Jesus Christ. The sign is of Christ crucified and risen, an identification with Christ and the body of Christ on earth. Making the sign and placing the sign in blessing, both by those presiding and by those in the assembly to one another, is

---

9. Andreopoulos, *The Sign of the Cross*, 92.
10. Andreopoulos, *The Sign of the Cross*, 11.
11. Andreopoulos, *The Sign of the Cross*, 13.

a means of mutual gospeling multisensorily. One two-year-old in the congregation I serve is eager to receive the sign of the cross on her forehead during the passing of the peace. She's not yet into words, but she does point to her forehead, and I know what that means and what she expects from me!

Movements and hand gestures are important modes of preaching multisensorily. I am not referring to what I call "perambulating preachers," who somehow seem to want to imitate late-night talk-show hosts—"Look, folks, no notes!" Little do they realize that some of the talk-show monologue is scripted and being projected on hidden teleprompters. The word of God is too weighty for a preacher to carry around with notes and anecdotes stored in his or her memory or loss thereof. There are a few preachers who can project the sermon's manuscript on their memories, yet for the rest of us the words preached are in front of us either on paper or on the transparent electronic tablets that are visible only to the preacher—or the President of the USA, or to anybody who wants to make sure that every word, carefully crafted, is delivered correctly. Presidents and preachers need to be accountable for their words—presidents accountable politically and preachers accountable to the Word of God. Physical movement to the pulpit or ambo signals to all who have ears to hear that what is to be heard is more than talk-show babble but intends to become, through the Holy Spirit in this assembly's hearing, the Word of God.

There also are hand and facial gestures that can communicate scolding and judgment or welcoming and gospeling. Then there are body movements that suggest discomfort or disorganization or affectations that hint of disingenuousness or insincerity or even that the preacher doesn't or can't believe what he or she is saying. Kimberly Long's *The Worshiping Body* carefully teaches the various qualities involved in the art of leading worship.

And then there is the movement in and of the assembly. Most churches are overpewed. Movement, particularly in churches of the Reformed tradition, often is restricted to entering and exiting, to sitting and standing in place. In the redesigned Episcopal Cathedral in Philadelphia, the assembly gathers around the font with its flowing water, moves to chairs at the pulpit for the Word read and preached, and then makes an offering and stands around the altar/table for the eucharist. Physical movement accompanies the liturgy. In predominantly African American assemblies, spontaneous body movements accompany the praying and singing. Clapping, not as applause to a performance, but as praise to God, breaks out from time to time. Dancing, not only by the "official dancers" but even by individuals in the assembly, is natural and unrehearsed. The offerings—yes, there are sometimes multiple offerings—are a steady stream of people walking to deacons holding big baskets and placing their gifts in the baskets. In other traditions it is customary for those wanting to commune to move physically either to stations where the bread and wine are given or to kneel at an altar rail to receive in the hand the bread and to drink from a common cup. (By the way, a cognitively impaired adult taught me the difference between "taking" communion and "receiving" communion. Anna always held out her two hands, right over left, to receive the bread of heaven.) All the movements are intrinsic to the liturgies and therefore are modes of gospeling multisensorily.

I once attended a megachurch purposely designed and orchestrated *not* to be and *not* to do what the cultured despisers of religion supposedly don't like. There were no symbols—no table, no font, not even a pulpit. To those presiders who didn't want to perambulate, a plexiglass lectern was carried in. Up front there was a band that played with more than ample amplification. The seating was theater style with the kind of individual comfy well-padded seats that are customary in the movies. The assembly did nothing except arrive and depart—no standing, no singing, no unison praying. The performers up front did everything for the passive assembly. When it came time for the offering, the presider apologized to the first-timers that the church didn't expect anybody to put anything in the plate. "Just sit back, and enjoy the band." I didn't! The only sense, sometimes seemingly bombarded, was my hearing.

When one of the senses is impaired, most often the other senses compensate. If one loses sight, either through disease, trauma, or even at birth, hearing and touch assume more prominent roles as receptors. Sight-impaired persons are able to develop a more acute sensitivity to sounds than sighted persons possess. They also develop a keen sense of touch, and learn how to read Braille and to perceive objects through the touches of a cane. Those with hearing loss compensate by a greater reliance on the sense of sight and learn to communicate by American Sign Language. Those with cognitive limitations often are more sensitive—as receiving impressions—multisensorily than many of us who are so sensorily deprived that we depend spiritually on what we hear or read. There are many more nuances to compensations for any impairments to the senses than in this oversimplification. The point is that those we diagnose as "impaired" may develop greater capacities for receiving the Word of God than those of us considered "normal."

Likewise, the same is true for persons suffering from dementias. Long after some no longer can recognize what day it is or remember what they had for lunch thirty minutes earlier, they still relate to the signs and actions of holy communion, they still join in praying the Lord's Prayer, and they still can sing by memory first stanzas of Christmas carols. Symbols are the last to go! Hear the last two stanzas of Bonar's hymn-prayer to Christ:

Too soon we rise, the symbols disappear.
The feast, though not the love, is past and gone;
the bread and wine remove, but you are here,
nearer than ever, still our shield and sun.

Feast after feast thus comes and passes by,
yet, passing, points to that glad feast above,
giving sweet foretaste of the festal joy,
the Lamb's great bridal feast of bless and love.

Christian worship, particularly in Protestant circles, in the American colonies during the seventeenth and eighteenth centuries was shaped considerably by both Puritan theology and the scarcity of resources for the building of gathering places. New England "meeting houses" were constructed for both worship and political functions. Calvinist trends in Europe to dismantle all symbols and images in the sixteenth century gave license to settlers on these shores to build houses of worship completely devoid of "popish" images and symbols. The end result was worship centered on a pulpit and an assembly whose role was primarily sedentary, to "sit," and auditory, to "hear" sermons and prayers spoken by the preacher. The assembly, if they were able to read and if hymnals were available, sometimes were led in singing a cappella by a precentor who sometimes "lined out" the words and tunes. Worship was predominantly a one-sensed, auditory experience, a model that quickly spread across the land by missionary and itinerant preachers. Worship consisted of a sermon prefaced by some singing, readings, and prayers and appended with a short closing benediction. Even today the space where the assembly gathers is sometimes referred to as the "auditorium"—that is, a place to "hear," from the Latin *audio*. And the assembly also sometimes is referred to the "audience," from the same Latin stem but ratcheted-up in intensity—and volume—through the influences and appeals of the entertainment industry.

Literacy, such a necessity for liturgical expressions in today's worship—regardless of style—has a tendency to flatten the biblical metaphors and the Christian symbols that identified and nourished the church for centuries. There was a time—and I will not provide dates—when it was not necessary for people to read and write. Scribes in the days before and after Jesus were the "readers" and "writers" who were called upon and employed to vocalize for hearers what they saw as alphabetic symbols and to translate into those symbols what the speaker wished to communicate. Reading was not necessary until after Gutenberg's invention of the printing press. That means that three-fourths of the assemblies in Christian history did not need to read, and there are still cultural and liturgical settings in which the mode of gospeling and receiving the Word is primarily oral and aural, speaking and hearing. And for more than a millennium of that Christian experience, what was said and heard was in a different language from what the assemblies spoke and heard in home and marketplace.

So, the gospel was proclaimed multisensorily. Stained glass preached. It gospeled the sacred story of God's actions in Israel, in the life, death, resurrection, and ascension of Jesus, and in the apostolic community—and even how God was still speaking through the contemporaries when the windows were crafted. Other visual arts—sculpture, mosaics, paintings, frescoes, architecture—were employed to gospel the faith-story. Music—both instrumental and choral and combinations of both—enticed assemblies into the sacred mysteries. Architecture of baptisteries and churches invited the uninitiated and the faithful into a foretaste of heaven. Even gothic churches in Europe that were bombed out during World War II, such as the cathedral in Coventry, England, and the Kaiser Wilhelm Memorial Church in Berlin, Germany, still proclaim in their ruins multisensorily the horrors of war. Yet, in both instances, beside the ruins, modern sacred spaces have arisen that, like those they replaced, gospel the resurrection and the life.

It has become trendy and almost de rigueur in some traditions to install projection screens or huge video monitors on which to project or electronically produce images. Supposedly these are modern adaptations of the visuals created in stained glass and other visual arts. Projected images can be faithful modes of preaching visually, but they need to be carefully chosen, artfully appropriate, liturgically and homiletically integrated, and, most importantly, technically well executed. This medium is not appropriate for the projection of texts and music for the assembly's participation. The computer's font needs to be too large for more than a few lines to appear at a time. Hymns and Psalms are not sing-alongs led by somebody with a microphone glued to his or her lips. That's entertainment, not worship of God. Nor are screens an appropriate means for announcements for current or upcoming events in the church, even before the liturgy begins. That's equivalent to

TV commercials, not gospel proclamation. I have seen the best and the worst and everything in between. When the screens and/or large flat-screen monitors are architecturally integrated into the building and all of the issues I delineated above are followed, the images used sparingly without drawing attention to themselves can be appropriate means of gospeling. Yet, most congregations do not have the resources, both human and material, to invest in what is needed for images to be equal to or even better than the multisensory means of gospeling that for nearly two thousand years have immersed people in the splendor of God in the liturgy, and in those moments when a solitary person kneels for prayer and the church building itself gospels multisensorily. Moreover, when the plug is pulled, the electronic image is gone. In that sense, electronically produced images are artificial and transitory. I was forced to experience one experiment in which an old roll-up screen was placed on a coffee table in the middle of the chancel of a large church and a less-than-experienced teenage technician projected the texts of songs to which the assembly was invited to sing along. God and that assembly of the people of God deserved the best that mortals could offer, not some gimmicky attempt to be "contemporary," supposedly to appeal to certain tastes. A pastor of an urban congregation that includes a group of young professionals tells of a conversation around installing video screens in the church. The sentiments of some of these were captured in the comments of one of them: "We spend all our hours at work staring at video screens. We don't want to do that on Sunday!"

Several years ago I was driving home from officiating at a funeral for a retired clergy and attending a long meeting with students in discernment for ministry. I stopped at a McDonald's along the highway. As I was returning to my car, I perceived that there was someone following me. "Father" [I was wearing a clerical collar], "may I talk with you about something?" I abruptly turned around and found a young man probably in his late twenties, well groomed, dressed in plaid shorts and a colored T-shirt. I half-heartedly said, "Yes," although I had been made cynical by too many such requests that amounted to panhandling for money, but this fellow seemed different. "I did a terrible thing," he said. "I stole money from my employer. I paid him back, and he forgave me, but I can't get over what a terrible thing I did. I can't forgive myself. I went to confession, and I know that God forgives me, but I can't forgive myself. Can you *do* something (italics mine) for me that will help me forgive myself?" We spent far more than several minutes there in that parking-lot pastoral-care session. He poured out his soul. I prayed with him, and gave him the Trinitarian blessing with the placing of the sign of the cross on his forehead. "Thank you, thank you! That's what I needed," and he hurried off to his car and I to mine.

9

Preaching *Engagingly*

*Now when they heard this, they were cut to the heart and said
to Peter and to the other apostles, "What should we do?"*

—Acts 2:37

*With great power the apostles gave their testimony to the res-
urrection of the Lord Jesus, and great grace was upon them all.*

—Acts 4:33

My wife and I took our two grandchildren, then age eleven
and thirteen, on a ten-day visit to Germany. The purpose
was to enable them to experience a different language and culture and to engage local people in more than touristic settings.
There were several preconditions, one of which was that there
was to be no cell-phoning and texting during the ten days in
Germany. To guarantee compliance, their Internet connections
were by prior agreement temporarily disengaged during the
immersion experience. The Internet hiatus was transformative. They actually *talked* with people and engaged in human
eye-to-eye contact with strangers, some of whom soon became
friends. It was a wonderful experience for them and for their
grandparents.

The Internet enables people to be connected to others at
distances where some of us are old enough to remember that

the only economically viable method of contacting people on the other side of the world was by mail—now prefaced by a new adjective, "snail." Nevertheless, today's social media create distancing in human relationships. Many of us are concerned that people—not just teenagers—are becoming socially challenged and incapable of establishing the relationships that build character, shape intimacy, and are necessary for commerce and the commonweal. For more than a half-century TV preachers have been creating electronic "parishioners," yet there can be no sense of assembly when people are engaged solely by TV screens and computer monitors. No wonder many people no longer want to be "preached at." I am quite sure that there is more texting going on Sunday mornings in churches than we preachers are willing to admit. Little hand-held screens to see electronic texts have replaced ears to hear!

In a previous chapter we considered "assembly" as the primary context of preaching. Now the adverbial discussion centers on preaching in an assembly *engagingly*. And, as discussed earlier, "preaching" is not restricted to what happens during a sermon; gospeling occurs throughout the assembly's total engagement with the Word of God.

Much has been written on the subject of "engaging preaching," and "engaging worship," some of which approaches worship and preaching from the perspective of performance theory. Yet, to me, there is a difference between "engaging preaching" associated with a type of sermonizing and the *art* of preaching *engagingly* within the more encompassing doing of the whole liturgy *engagingly*. Even the best attempt to preach an engaging sermon in a service of worship that is a tangle of disjuncted songs, preacher-prayers, musical performances, and chats with kids, fails to engage at more than a superficial level. The sermon becomes focused on the preacher and his or her homiletical talents. However, preaching a sermon engagingly is but a part of an assembly's doing *liturgy engagingly*. And that involves more than preachers and presiders. The whole assembly is engaged in gospeling engagingly.

I have no talent for or interest in golf. My attempts at

playing golf decades ago ended on a hot summer day by my throwing the clubs into the trunk of my car and vowing never to try again. They got sold at a garage sale. I worshiped last year in a church in a rather upscale community where supposedly most of the more able-bodied in the assembly were adept at playing golf. The preacher started with some references to golf-jargon that got some chuckles from some of the folks. But I had no clue as to what she was talking about, and her continued attempts at golf metaphors simply didn't engage me. I assume she was trying—apparently successfully with some in the assembly—to preach an engaging sermon, but it didn't engage me with the Scripture. The organist positioned front and center with his doctoral hood prominently exposed to the assembly played with precision. The large choir directed by another "hooded" person sang beautifully, but nothing seemed to fit together homiletically and liturgically. I went empty away.

As of this writing I also am writing a sermon for this coming Sunday. The Gospel for the Second Sunday of Easter in all three years of the Revised Common Lectionary cycle is John 20:19–31—Thomas's engagement with the risen Christ. Juxtaposed between the reading of the Gospel and the sermon will be a wonderful contemporary hymn by Thomas Troeger set to a haunting tune, KEDRON, from Amos Pilsbury's 1799 *United States Sacred Harmony*:

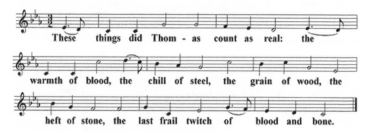

These things did Thom - as count as real: the warmth of blood, the chill of steel, the grain of wood, the heft of stone, the last frail twitch of blood and bone.

2. The vision of his sceptic mind
   was keen enough to make him blind
   to any unexpected act
   too large for his small world of fact.

3. His reasoned certainties denied
   that one could live when one had died,
   until his fingers read like Braille
   the markings of the spear and nail.

4. May we, O God, by grace believe,
   and thus the risen Christ receive,
   whose raw imprinted hands reached out
   and beckoned Thomas from his doubt.[1]

The hymn serves as a hermeneutical transition between Scripture and sermon. The first three stanzas begin the process of recontextualizing that will continue in the sermon. The fourth stanza is a prayer that will lead directly into the sermon that I have titled "Beyond Doubt and Reasoned Certainties."

Yet, the homiletical engagement begins earlier with a prayer for illumination prior to the reading of the Scriptures:

Leader: O God, who prompted holy apostles
          to proclaim the good news
          of Jesus' resurrection victory,
          grant that as we listen to their witness,
          the convincing power of your Holy Spirit
          will confirm our faith that Jesus is the Christ,
          and that through this faith
          we may receive new life in his name.
All: **Amen.**[2]

The lector presides for the prayer and the reading of Acts 4:32–35. This prayer recontextualizes images in Acts 4:33 and John 20:30–31 and asks the Holy Spirit to actualize the Word of God in the reading and hearing of the texts and in the sermon that will follow. Images also appear in the call to worship:

1. © Oxford University Press 1984. Reproduced by permission of CopyCat Music Licensing LLC on behalf of Oxford University Press. All rights reserved.
2. From: F. Russell Mitman, *Immersed in the Splendor of God: Resources for Worship Renewal* (Cleveland: Pilgrim, 2005), 100.

Leader: Alleluia! Christ is risen!

All: The Lord is risen indeed! Alleluia!

Leader: Blessed be the God and Father of our Lord Jesus Christ!

All: By his great mercy we have been born anew to a living hope through the resurrection of Jesus Christ from the dead! —1 Peter 1:3

and in the penitential act:

Call to Confession:

Leader: If then we have been raised with Christ,
let us set our hearts on the things of heaven
where Christ is
and put behind us the earthly things
in which we once walked. —paraphrased from Colossians 3:1–5

Please be seated.

Confession of sin and Kyrie:

Leader: Let us pray.

Leader: O Creator God, by whose hand we are made
and in whose hands we are held,

**All: how questioning is our faith
in your faithfulness,
how wavering our trust in your trustfulness!**

Leader: Lord, have mercy on us.

All: Lord, have mercy on us.

Silence

Leader: O Christ, through whose pierced hands and side
we are set free from bondage to sin and death,

All: **how slow are we to believe news**
              almost too good to be true,
              how reluctant to share it with others!

Leader: Christ, have mercy on us.

All: **Christ, have mercy on us.**

Silence

Leader: O Holy Spirit, whose commissioning power
              is handed over to us,

All: **how afraid we are to accept**
              the call to righteousness,
              how ashamed of holiness!

Leader: Lord, have mercy on us.

All: **Lord, have mercy on us.**

Silence

Leader: O holy and undivided Trinity, One God,

All: **have mercy on us, pardon our sin,**
              and grant us your peace. Amen.

Thus, by the time the assembly encounters the readings of Scripture themselves, there is an Easter motif that already has been running through the liturgy. The sermon continues the preaching that begins with the opening "Alleluia!" and will go on through the final thanksgiving that repeats the passage from 1 Peter 1:3 with which the service begins.

It is clear that not everyone will be "with it" at every expression throughout the homiletical/liturgical event, as a director of music reminded me years ago. Different individuals in the assembly are engaged differently—hence the need for the preaching to engage multisensorily as discussed in the previous chapter. Yet, preaching engagingly is not achieved through some artificially imposed homiletical and liturgical techniques. Preaching engagingly, as the theme of this book suggests, is an *art* of engaging the assembly: imaginatively, inclusively, believably, carefully, and gracefully.

Imagination is a gift of God that is given to everyone, not in equal measure, yet a given that each person has. Unfortunately the training we have received at the hands of a left-over Enlightenment pedagogy has suppressed the imagination in most adults and even tainted the word: "It's all just in your imagination." In other words, what is in your imagination supposedly is not real. Younger children still possess the power of imagination in fuller measure. I suggest that as worship leaders we spend time with children to unlearn our bad habits of mind and to rediscover the gift that God has given us.

Many times the Scriptures themselves invite us into imagining. For example, in the encounter of Jesus with Thomas in the Gospel of John we considered above, John entices us to engage our imaginations in the very first sentence: "When it was evening on that day, the first day of the week, and the doors of the house where the disciples had met were locked . . . , Jesus came and stood among them and said, 'Peace be with you'" (John 20:19). Imagine it being the evening of the day of Jesus's resurrection; imagine locked doors, implying that no one could enter the normal way; imagine then, Jesus standing among them and speaking the peace to them. John wants us to imagine the setting in order for us to be engaged by the proclamation of Jesus's resurrection, and to imagine ourselves behind locked doors. A sermon on the Gospel for Easter 2 may start out with: "Imagine it is evening on the same day Jesus was resurrected from death. Imagine the doors of the house where the disciples are meeting are locked, and Jesus comes and stands there among them. . . ." The gospel narrative itself invites the assembly into imagining and the preacher into gospeling engagingly.

Not every biblical text is a narrative. Yet, there are images and metaphors in texts that invite imagining, and there are everyday experiences that invite engaging the assembly with the biblical texts. I remember a sermon preached by Fred Craddock more than twenty years ago on Revelation 3:1. ("And to the angel of the church in Sardis write: These are the words of him who has the seven spirits of God and the seven stars: 'I know your works; you have a name of being alive, but you are dead.'") In his homespun style Fred related driving with his wife, Letty, by one of the churches he had served earlier in his ministry. The parking lot was full, and there were signs that the church was very much alive. However, Fred and Letty discovered very quickly that the congregation had disbanded and the building had been sold and turned into a restaurant. In vivid detail he walked the assembly through the restaurant, contrasting the various appointments when the sanctuary had been used for worship with what now was happening in the restaurant. All of us in that assembly were engaged in accompanying Fred imaginatively through that church turned into a restaurant. And then, suddenly the text emerged: "You have a name of being alive, but you are dead," and the proclamation: "Your church is dead!" Most of us in the assembly were parish pastors, and to hear, "Your church is dead," as Luke reports in Peter's Pentecost sermon, we were "stung in the heart" with gospel questioning.

It was Fred Craddock and others—too many in that great company of preachers to name—who broke the conventional mold of preaching in the last quarter of the twentieth century. One of those writing during that renaissance of preaching, who also has been my preaching mentor, Paul Scott Wilson, said: "A number of recent developments suggest that there is a shift taking place in biblical preaching that amounts to a new emphasis on imagination and a different understanding of it. . . . Form and content vary in accordance with the form and content of the biblical text. In short the sermon or homily is being upheld as a form of art dedicated to the opening up of God's living word for today."[3] Thomas Troeger wrote at about the same time: "We commonly associate the imagination with illusion and deception. 'It is all in your imagination,' we say. But imagination is leading us to an acknowledgment of real-

---

3. Paul Scott Wilson, *Imagination of the Heart: New Understandings in Preaching* (Nashville: Abingdon, 1988), 22–23.

ity, not an escape from it. Of course it is not imagination on its own, but imagination encouraged by the Spirit, disciplined by Scripture, informed by the wisdom of the homiletical city, and energized by the need of the world."[4] Note how Troeger engages imaginatively a singing assembly with the metaphors: "His [Thomas's] reasoned certainties denied that one could live when one had died, until his fingers read like Braille the markings of the spear and nail." People can imagine, even though they themselves are not physically sight-impaired, feeling the dots of Braille and experiencing the gospel's spear that pierced Jesus's side and the nails that hung him.

Walter Brueggemann has said, "I want to consider preaching as a poetic construal of an alternative world. The purpose of such preaching is to cherish the truth, to open the truth from its pervasive reductionism in our society, to break from the fearful rationality that keeps the news from being new."[5] He continues:

> The community waits for the text that may be a tent for the spirit. . . . But if the text is to claim authority it will require neither the close reasoning of a canon lawyer, nor the precision of a technician, but it will require an artist to render the text in quite fresh ways, so that the text breaks life open among the baptized as it never has before. . . . This precious moment of speech . . . is not time for cleverness or novelty. It is not time for advice or scolding or urging, because the text is not any problem-solving answer or a flat, ideological agent that can bring resolve. This moment of speech is a poetic rendering in a community that has come all too often to expect nothing but prose. . . . When the text has been reduced to prose, life becomes so prosaic that there is a dread dullness that besets the human spirit.[6]

4. Thomas H. Troeger, *Imagining a Sermon* (Nashville: Abingdon, 1990), 28.

5. Walter Brueggemann, *Finally Comes the Poet: Daring Speech for Proclamation* (Minneapolis: Augsburg Fortress, 1989), 6.

6. Brueggemann, *Finally Comes the Poet*, 9.

Brueggemann adds that preaching is "an artistic moment in which the words are concrete but open, close to our life but moving out to new angles of reality. . . . The preacher listens to the biblical text, which is a long-standing conversation. The preacher listens to the life of the people, which is always an ongoing conversation. . . . The preacher does the imaginative act of rendering in words the conversation for both parties. . . . The preacher speaks for the community. The preacher then dares to speak for God."[7]

Troeger's imaging of the story of "doubting" Thomas, quoted above, exemplifies preaching engagingly whereby the assembly is drawn through powerful metaphors from biblical text into gospel Word. Yes, the genre is rhymed poetry meant to be sung; but it is more. Thomas becomes the archetype for every human being wavering in trust and uncertain in faith. The reading and hearing of Scripture, the corporate singing of the hymn, and the preaching of the sermon all juxtaposed with each other merge themselves into a unified act of gospeling: "Today this scripture has been fulfilled in your hearing"—and praying and singing. And, it asks, "Whose is the skeptic mind and what are the reasoned certainties?"

Troeger's hymn illustrates also that preaching engagingly is preaching *carefully*. Note how every word is chosen not only to fit the meter and rhyme but also to proclaim the gospel's power. Truly this homiletical and liturgical act is, in Brueggemann's analogy, the "poetic construal of an alternative reality," not simply because it is poetry but because it becomes in the assembly's singing the gospel of resurrection reality. To preach engagingly is to be aware that each word preached embodies sacramental reality, and the choosing of each word becomes, through the Holy Spirit, a vessel of God's alternatives—too weighty a task for off-the-cuff extemporizing. An assembly gathered with the desire, "We want to see Jesus," deserves far more than talk-show entertainment blab. Luke reports that those who heard Peter's Pentecost sermon were "cut to the heart,"

7. Brueggemann, *Finally Comes the Poet*, 76–77.

translated literally from the Greek, "stung in the heart." To attempt gospeling engagingly involves choosing words carefully.

The often-quoted dictum attributed to St. Francis of Assisi: "Preach the gospel; use words if necessary" prompted a rejoinder by Mark Galli: "Preach the gospel—use actions when necessary; use words always."[8] He explains:

> "Preach the gospel; use words if necessary" goes hand in hand with a postmodern assumption that words are finally empty of meaning. It subtly denigrates the high value that the prophets and Jesus and Paul put on preaching. Of course we want our actions to match our words as much as possible. But the gospel is a message, news about an event and a person upon which the history of the planet turns. . . . Words used cheaply, thoughtlessly are worse than no words at all.

Galli goes on to refer to an article, "Letting Words Do Their Work," by Marilyn McEntyre. McEntyre writes:

> In an environment permeated with large-scale, well-funded deceptions, the business of telling the truth, and caring for the words we need for that purpose, is more challenging than ever before. . . . That difficulty makes it urgent that we learn new strategies of truth-telling in the interests of waging peace and delivering the good news that is bigger than the bad news—indeed, in the interests of survival.
>
> It is hard to tell the truth these days, because the varieties of untruth are so many, so pervasive, and so well disguised. Lies are hard to identify when they come in the form of apparently innocuous imprecisions, socially acceptable slippages, hyperboles posing as enthusiasm, or well-placed propaganda. . . . All of us are called to seek truth and follow after it, to do justice, to love mercy, and to walk humbly with our God. Caring for the words we speak and testing

8. Mark Galli, "*Speak* the Gospel: Use Deeds When Necessary," *Christianity Today*, May 21, 2009.

the words we hear are indispensable dimensions of that vocation.[9]

Emailing and texting not only have played havoc with English spelling and grammar but have also allowed anger and other emotions that we would never display face to face to escape civil restraint. The old children's adage "Sticks and stones may break my bones, but words can never hurt me" is very wrong. Words can and do hurt deeply, and words that have slipped too easily from the tongues of some preachers have inflicted wounds for life. Words have great power to engage for good or evil, and words intended to be vehicles of divine judgment and grace need to be chosen ever so carefully.

Extemporaneity in preaching can easily result in unintended consequences and be both the excuse for and the result of the lack of careful preparation needed for an assembly's authentic engagement with the gospel. Some politicians have learned too late that an extemporaneous slip of the tongue can cause the loss of an election!

Preaching engagingly and carefully involves, in the previous quote from Walter Ong, the art of oralizing texts. A sermon is an act of oralizing words carefully chosen to engage the assembly aurally. Martin Luther's famous dictum: "Die Kirche ist ein Mundhaus, nicht ein Federhaus" (The church is a "mouth" house, not a "pen" house—"pen" as in a quill) became a cornerstone of Reformation preaching as an acoustical act. That often-quoted Lutherism comes from a sermon he preached in 1521 on Matthew 21:1-9 for the First Sunday of Advent (Jesus's arrival in Bethphage). The quote continues: "For since Christ's Advent, the Gospel preached orally what was hidden textually in books. So also it is the nature of the New Testament and the Gospel that it be preached and be delivered with lively voice."[10] Ironically, the text of this sermon that Luther deliv-

---

9. Marilyn McEntyre, "Letting Words Do Their Work," *Christianity Today*, September 22, 2009.

10. Friedrich Franke, ed., *Dr. Martin Luther's sämtliche Schriften*,

ered orally—surely with "lively" voice!—is available nearly five hundred years later because he first wrote it with a quill pen! In other words, he preached from a manuscript; that is, he oralized a text he had written.

The church as "Mundhaus" became a practicality in Colonial and Revolutionary America. Since church buildings frequently were the largest gathering places in most cities and towns in the USA through the nineteenth century, they served as mouth houses for large civic assemblies. Old South Meeting House in Boston, built in 1729, was and still is such a mouth house that has been the site of public debates about the American Revolution, the planning of the Boston Tea Party, as well as debate on the issues of slavery, Abolitionism, the Vietnam War, and the Iraq War. The German Reformed Church (now First United Church of Christ) in Easton, Pennsylvania, was the site in 1777 of meetings between the peace commissioners appointed by Congress and representatives of various Indian nations. Thomas Paine, the famous Revolutionary pamphleteer and author of "Common Sense," served as secretary to the commissioners at these meetings. The civil rights movement in the 1960s under the leadership of the Rev. Martin Luther King Jr. started in mouth houses such as Ebenezer Baptist Church in Atlanta, Georgia, where he was preacher, pastor, and teacher.

To preach engagingly—"with lively voice," as the first Martin Luther said and his namesake did—means crafting sermon and liturgy so that preacher and assembly can oralize the texts. Paul Scott Wilson says:

> After often eighteen years of academic training for ministry, most of it for the page, our theological writing tends not to imitate speech; rather, our theological speech normally imitates writing. Speech that imitates academic writing often sounds like a lecture, or an essay being read. . . . Once we conceive of preaching as an oral event, we begin to shift our

vol. 11: *Die Evangelienpredigten* (Leipzig: E. Schimmel, 1846), 49 (translation mine).

ways of thinking. Instead of composing with the eye for the page, we begin to compose with the ear for oral delivery and aural reception, attentive to various needs of the listeners.[11]

As I compose on the word processor and see the words emerging on the video monitor, I speak them aloud, often changing words as I am speaking them so that later they can be spoken and heard orally in sermon and liturgy. After years of being exposed to this practice, my family began to overlook that Dad is in his study talking to himself again!

Corporate speaking in the assembly necessitates phrases that can be said together, essentially in one breath. Note, for instance, the way in which the following penitential prayer is written and printed to facilitate oral speech. It is based on the text of Isaiah 55:1–9, which is appointed in the Revised Common Lectionary for Lent 3 in Year C:

O God, whose thoughts are not our thoughts,
    and whose ways are not our ways;
we confess the rebel thoughts
    that sever us from our dependence on you,
and we acknowledge the disobedient ways
    that lead us from your paths
        of holiness and righteousness.
There is a vast difference between where we are
    and where you intend us to be.
So we ask for your unbounded love to find us in our sin,
    to rescue us from ourselves,
    to lead us to the living waters that restore,
    and to give us the bread of life
    that fills us with good things;
        through the grace of Jesus Christ.
Amen.[12]

11. Paul Scott Wilson, *The Practice of Preaching* (Nashville: Abingdon, 1995), 47–48.

12. Mitman, *Immersed in the Splendor of God*, 93.

The same is true in preaching sermons engagingly. More will be said in the following chapter. What needs saying here is that allowing an assembly to be engaged by the Word of God necessitates crafting *ahead of Sunday morning* how the words will be written in the sermon manuscript so that the preacher, oralizing the words scripted, will not be *reading* but will be *preaching Christ* live-ly. By the way, the famous "I Have a Dream" speech of Dr. Martin Luther King Jr.—which was really a sermon—was scripted, even though King, like any preacher caught up in the moment of truth, would depart from the text. There is a difference between a carefully scripted sermon with breathing room for the Holy Spirit to engage the assembly and a talk-show-type monologue of off-the-cuff remarks designed to entertain "the audience."

When Martin the monk urged preaching "mit lebendigen Stimme," which is translated as "with lively voice," perhaps the English "lively" is just a bit too casual and dispassionate. "Lively" conjures up synonyms such as "animated" and "sprightly," even in my computer's thesaurus: "boisterous," "merry," "snappy," "spanking," and "zippy." (It seems the synonyms get more ridiculous the farther down the alphabet you go!) Yet, sadly, some of us have suffered through sermons that were supposed to be any or all of the above! No wonder some folks have quit church! Luther's "mit lebendigen Stimme" is better translated as "with a voice that is alive." *Lebendig* in German comes from the verb *leben*, "to live." The voice of the one preaching intends to engage the assembly with the Word of *life*.

That raises the issue that preaching engagingly is to preach *authentically*. The question is not "Was the sermon snappy?" but "Did the preacher preach authentically?" Notice that I did not say "convincingly." To "convince" still lingers in the rhetoric of lectures or revival meetings. The synonyms for "authentically" come up as "faithfully," "reliably," "responsibly." I will add "living-ly." Are the words preached faithful to the gospel? Are they responsible to an authority greater than the preacher's "*I* believe," or "in *my* opinion"? The question is not, "Can I trust the preacher?," but "Can I trust the Word?" "Are the words being preached by a voice living the Word, and can *I* live the Word?" The same question can be asked of the whole worship event: "Does the liturgy live?" and "Can I live the liturgy?"

Luther's translation of the Bible into German was intended to enable assemblies to be engaged with the Word of God not only as texts that were read aloud but also through preaching, prayers, and the sacraments. He also produced a redaction of the Latin Mass into German. His project of translating the Bible into the vernacular involved asking people how they would say the words of the texts in everyday life. It was an attempt to engage worshiping assemblies authentically—in literary constructs that not only were authentic to the texts in their ancient languages but mirrored also the ways of speaking that were indigenous to common people. A byproduct of creating a German translation of the Bible for worship and devotion was that it brought about a defining of what constituted a common German language in a day when many dialects in many separate principalities made it almost impossible for some German-speakers to understand other German-speakers. Even the former German Democratic Republic in 1983—before the fall of the regime—issued a postage stamp honoring Luther, not for his theological and ecclesial attempts at reformation, but for the publication of his translation of the Bible printed in 1541 that provided a common literary standard in the German language.

"Mit lebendigen Stimme" in days before the advent of electronic sound amplification meant the ability "to project" one's voice. Colonial-era pulpits—or reproductions of them—were elevated high so those assembled could see the preacher above the high box-like pews that were needed in cold winters. Pulpits also were fitted out with a wooden canopy over the head of the preacher that acted like a sounding board to amplify the sound. In order to be heard in large churches with unfriendly acoustics some preachers developed what sometimes was called a "stained-glass voice." Men with booming bass voices and those who had naturally or could acquire a Scottish or British accent were rewarded with the "prize pulpits," while thin tenor or soprano voices were not given a second interview. Some preachers tried to mimic well-known pulpiteers, and some seminarians were schooled in exercises to overcome foreign or regional accents. The end result was not a "living voice" but affectations that raised questions of authenticity—not only of the person preaching but also of the words being preached, prompting some off-handed gossip: "Is the preacher for real?"

The same can be said regarding the reading of Scripture in worship. Like preaching a sermon, reading Scripture, that is, oralizing a text, is an art that can be taught and learned and practiced. There are some who teach that Scripture should be read without affect, that is, without putting any expression in the oralizing—straightforward without any hint of interpreting the text. On the other hand, I have been subjected to those—primarily preachers—who try to dramatize the text and thus put too much of their own personalities into the oralization. To me, the reader gets in the way of the text, and his or her oralizing the text begs the question of authenticity. I maintain that authentic reading of Scripture lies somewhere between the two poles—letting the text be itself but also allowing the inherent emotions in the text to come to expression without affectation. By the way, long Scripture narratives such as the stories of the man born blind and the raising of Lazarus invite juxtaposing the reading of segments of the texts with homiletical reflections on each segment. Scripture and sermon are integrated dialogically.

At the other end of the authenticity scale are those who try to "get real" with people by engaging in homiletical chitchat as though talking with a long-lost friend on the telephone, sharing jokes and personal stories. Preaching engagingly has no room for either affected discourse or flippant babble. Nor, somewhere off the charts, do sermons that come across like the reading aloud of a footnoted PhD thesis or a journal article about a latest archeological dig in Palestine. Preaching engagingly is inviting people into a corporate conversation with a God whose ways are not our ways yet who comes incarnate in human ways and words and actions to entice humans into a sacred mystery that provokes the soul to say, "O my God!"

To preach engagingly is—in summary of all that has been said in this and previous chapters—to preach *passionately.* "With great power," Luke writes in Acts, "the apostles gave their testimony to the resurrection of the Lord Jesus, and great grace was upon them all" (Acts 4:33). The Greek word translated as "power" in English is *dynamis,* and much has been said and written about what authors and writers consider "dynamic" preaching. The Greek word translated as "testimony" is *martyrion,* and images of those whose witness and belonging to Christ has brought them to a martyr's death span two thousand years from Stephen in the first century to the victims of genocide in too many places in the twenty-first century. What jumps out of this one-sentence text from Acts is that those who preached Christ resurrected preached *passionately.* Preaching passionately is preaching engagingly with all one's heart and soul and mind and strength—with all one's being—actively, engagingly, living-ly, authentically, carefully, lovingly.

My doctoral mentor, Dow Edgerton, wrote at the conclusion of his work on hermeneutics, which he titled *The Passion of Interpretation*:

> Passion is a word of many senses. Passion has to do with love, hate, desire, and hunger. Passion is intensity and determination. Passion is power and the source of power. Passion is vocation and calling. Passion is giving oneself over to something outside oneself. Passion is the object toward which one's life is turned. For the Christian church, of course, the word has a special sense. Passion is the suffering of Christ, in the garden and on the cross. It is the suffering, also, of those in whom our imaginations see it all—not again—but for the first time. To speak of passion in this sense is to speak of the cost of love . . . bearing in one's body and spirit the cost of love, being changed by the cost of love, changed by love, changed for love, changed to love.[13]

13. W. Dow Edgerton, *The Passion of Interpretation* (Louisville: Westminster John Knox, 1992), 143–44.

Preaching passionately involves all the above.

When I am forced to list my "occupation" on a form, I write "retired." If I were asked to indicate my "vocation," I would write "preacher." I am retired in the sense that I am now an annuitant. But in my vocational vocabulary there is no retirement. When I became an annuitant after eighteen years of serving as an overseer of congregations, I became an active preacher and teacher, preaching in an assembly every Sunday—except for a few vacations. Every Monday I encounter the texts appointed for the following Sunday. It is not my first go-round with these texts, yet each Monday it is as if I am being encountered by the Word again for the first time. I discover that the passion for preaching is woven into the texts themselves, and that, instead of me trying to find some sermonic theme in the texts, the texts engage me. The art of preaching passionately is allowing the inherent passion in the texts—with all its senses and emotions—to engage itself homiletically in the sermon and liturgically in the whole worship event. And thus, preaching becomes passion-driven. It is, in Dow's words, "giving oneself over to something outside oneself."

And such "giving oneself over to something outside oneself" is the vocation that engages every baptized Christian. To preach Christ passionately is the commission that is marked with the sign of the cross in every baptism on every person immersed in sacramental grace and infused in the passion of Christ. As an orchestra of many different instruments playing in ensemble, every assembly is engaged in ensemble in a common act of preaching as together they do liturgy. Everyone is a preacher offering a diversity of voices in unison and in harmony as together they give themselves to a mystery outside themselves.

And each takes his or her voice out the church door as Christ sends them to engage others in the mystery of Christ. *Ita missa est* is the ancient traditional ending of the Roman mass, and it is from the *missa* that the mass gets its name. Generally it is translated in English versions as "Go forth, the Mass is ended." However, *missa* has roots in the Latin word for "send."

So, some conclude that it means, "Go, you are sent." The traditional response is *Deo gratias*, "thanks be to God." Some liturgies render the dismissal, "Go in peace. Serve the Lord," coupled with the response, "Thanks be to God." Regardless of how the dismissal is framed, the liturgical intention is a sending with a homiletical intention to gospel Christ in daily engagements with others. Preaching doesn't stop at the church door with a final handshake. In fact, when we step out into the world, Christ is already there, inviting, "Follow me."

10

*Preaching **Doxologically***

May the God of steadfastness and encouragement grant you to live in harmony with one another, in accordance with Christ Jesus, so that together you may with one voice glorify the God and Father of our Lord Jesus Christ.

—Romans 15:5–6

In shaping what this chapter intends, I searched for several adverbs as a title. First I tried on "musically," for there are a number of musical concepts that are indigenous to the homiletical and liturgical arts. Yet, "musically" was not inclusive enough. Neither was "artistically," although, as we shall see, there are many artistic theories that can be translated into ways of preaching. Even "architecturally" could be included: certainly church buildings "preach," "proclaim," and "communicate," sometimes for better or worse. All, however, seemed aspects of a more overarching and inclusive theme. British theologian Geoffrey Wainwright in the title of his extensive volume, *Doxology: The Praise of God in Worship, Doctrine, and Life*,[1] offers to me a title for this chapter, "Preaching Doxologically." Immediately to many accustomed to church life, "doxol-

1. Geoffrey Wainwright, *Doxology: The Praise of God in Worship, Doctrine, and Life* (New York: Oxford University Press, 1980).

ogy" conjures up what has gotten to be called "*the* doxology," those oversung words of Thomas Ken penned in 1674 to music composed by Louis Bourgeois for the Genevan Psalter of 1551. There are many, many other doxologies in both Old and New Testaments and in the liturgical history of the church. Certain liturgical traditions prescribe the weekly singing of the "Gloria in Excelsis" ("Glory to God in the highest"), known as the "greater doxology," and the "Gloria Patri" ("Glory to the Father"), known as the "lesser doxology." The latter frequently is added as a Trinitarian conclusion to the singing or speaking of one of the 150 Psalms.

The root words of the English word "doxology" are the Greek noun *doxa* ("glory," "splendor," "radiance") and the verb *doxazō* ("glorify," "praise," "honor"), plus *logos* ("word") or *legein* ("speaking"). Although most English dictionaries admit "doxological" and "doxologically" as the legitimate adjective and adverb forms, it is hard to find adequate definitions and synonyms for them. The Internet offers blogs on "sermon doxologies." I assume these are pithy sermon-closers, yet nothing substantive is offered about *preaching* doxologically.

Instead, let me give an illustration. I recently participated in an ecumenical worship service. During the offertory the choir sang some very lively music as each worshiper was ushered to the basket where we gave our offerings. Some people danced, some people sang. The atmosphere truly was doxological. Then, somewhat abruptly, the organist introduced the offertory response, and the assembly began to sing, "Praise God from whom all blessings flow . . ." like a funeral dirge. We did not sing "the doxology" doxologically! Yet, I also have been a participant in worship services in which those same words truly were sung doxologically, that is, praiseworthily, heartily, joyfully, gloriously.

"Doxology" generally is associated with music and singing. Without detouring into music psychology, it can be said that words articulated in song engage an emotional dimension that is not possible through speaking those same words alone. Assemblies regularly speak either corporately or responsively the words of Psalm 100: "Make a joyful noise to the Lord with gladness; come into his presence with singing." Something else is proclaimed and received when the same verse of Psalm 100 is sung corporately to a tune such as GENEVAN 134, commonly known as OLD HUNDREDTH: "All people that on earth do dwell, sing to the Lord with cheerful voice." This metrical setting from the sixteenth century is quite different from the other thousands of tunes to which these words have been sung in thousands of languages ever since their Hebrew origins as a doxology of thanksgiving some three thousand years ago.

I am fully aware that there are some people who do not sing either in church or in the shower, either because they don't like to sing or believe they can't sing or were told sometime in their youth that they shouldn't sing. Yet, except for those who physically cannot articulate a sound with their vocal cords, everyone can make a noise, even a joyful noise! I am constantly amazed at men, particularly, who stand mute while the assembly in church sings yet who belt out "Fly, Eagles, fly!" in a stadium or in a bar watching on TV as a certain football team from Philadelphia kicks and throws around an inflated ovaloid! Then there are the ten-year-old piano-lesson dropouts who vow that they never learned a thing musicologically. I am aware that there are some readers eager to skip the next few paragraphs on preaching doxologically in which I borrow some terms from musicology.

But first, the Westminster Shorter Catechism, in the language of 1647, wants to ask us: "What is the chief end of man?" and to remind us that "Man's chief end is to glorify God and to enjoy him forever." The fundamental purpose of human beings is doxological—"to glorify *God*"—and, "to enjoy," that is, "in joy" to *live* doxologically. To gospel (as a verb), to proclaim the *good* news liturgically and homiletically, is to preach *doxologically*. Pope Francis, in his encyclical *Evangelii Gaudium* (published in English as *The Joy of the Gospel*), grounds his call for a renewed evangelism not in some strategy for church growth but in the very heart of the gospel: joy. His opening sentences capture what I call his doxological agenda:

The joy of the gospel fills the hearts and lives of all who encounter Jesus. Those who accept his offer of salvation are set free from sin, sorrow, inner emptiness and loneliness. With Christ joy is constantly born anew. In this Exhortation I wish to encourage the Christian faithful to embark upon a new chapter of evangelization marked by this joy, while pointing out new paths for the Church's journey in the years to come.[2]

In his foreword to the encyclical Robert Barron traces a number of biblical references to joy, then asks the rhetorical question: "Why should we not also enter into this great stream of joy?"[3] Barron comments, "Pope Francis excoriates Christians who have turned 'into querulous and disillusioned pessimists,' 'sourpusses,' and whose lives 'seem like Lent without Easter.'"[4] "A church filled with the joy of the resurrection becomes a band of 'missionary disciples,' going out to the world with the good news."[5] He continues:

Ecclesial structures, liturgical precision, theological clarity, bureaucratic meetings, and so on are accordingly relativized in the measure that they are placed in the service of that more fundamental mission. The pope loves the liturgy, but if evangelical proclamation is the urgent need of the Church, "an ostentatious reoccupation with the liturgy" becomes a problem; a Jesuit, the pope loves the life of the mind, but if evangelical proclamation is the central concern of the Church, then a "narcissistic" and "authoritarian" doctrinal fussiness must be eliminated; a man of deep culture, Pope Francis loves the artistic heritage of the Church, but if evangelical proclamation is the fundamental mission, the Church cannot become "a museum piece."[6]

2. Pope Francis, *The Joy of the Gospel* (New York: Image, 2013), 5.
3. Robert Barron, "Foreword," *The Joy of the Gospel*, viii.
4. Barron, "Foreword," viii.
5. Barron, "Foreword," viii.
6. Barron, "Foreword," viii–ix.

Commentary on the pope's encyclical on evangelization might have been appropriate to chapter 4, on preaching evangelically. However, it is included here because of preaching's *doxological* intent. It is the fundamental *joy* of the gospel that grounds, empowers, and commissions preaching evangelically.

So, the questions need to arise before any sermon is preached and any liturgy is copied for the assembly's participation: Does this liturgy of which this sermon is part glorify *God*—even when the good news is both grace and judgment—and does, at the same time, the worship event in Charles Wesley's words, gospel (as a verb) the "joy of heaven to earth come down" and "fix in us [joy's] humble dwelling"? The joy of the gospel has no room for a preacher's cranky and scolding diatribe on any one of the culture's hot-button issues sprinkled with snippets from the book of Leviticus and prefixed and appended with repetitive praise choruses. Don Saliers says it eloquently: "The mystery of our life hid with Christ in God is sounded and offered back to us in the praying, the singing, the elements of bread and wine, the water, the oil, and the laying on of hands." [I would add: in the reading of Scripture and in the preaching of the sermon.] "When worship is faithful to its true subject—God incarnate and Spirit-giving—and relevant to our restlessness for God, it will restore us to joy and delight."[7]

Preaching doxologically involves preaching and doing liturgy *harmoniously*. Simply choosing a collection of well-known and beloved hymns that have nothing to do with the Scriptures and sermon creates a homiletical and liturgical disharmony that no well-crafted sermon can rectify. Preaching harmoniously involves the art of intentionally allowing the Scriptures to shape every expression in the liturgy as an organic whole, including sermon or homily, from beginning to end. This involves, as discussed previously, the process of crafting both liturgy and sermon simultaneously through the art, in Paul

7. Don E. Saliers, *Worship Come to Its Senses* (Nashville: Abingdon, 1996), 40.

Wilson's musical metaphor, of "transposing" the concern of the text into the "changed key"[8] of sermon and liturgy.

Likewise, those who serve as worship leaders—preachers, liturgists, lectors, ushers, acolytes, choirs, musicians—all need to be "on the same page." This does not preclude prayed-for intrusions of the Holy Spirit, but it does mean that leaders come to the worship prepared to lead. I learned from Gláucia Vasconcelos Wilkey that rehearsal, even on the part of the most able presiders and preachers, cannot be skipped. Training of worship leaders is necessary both to avoid embarrassment of the volunteers who offer themselves and to allow the assembly to offer to God doxologically their sacrifice of praise and thanksgiving. Everyone participating in liturgical and homiletical leadership in the church I serve receives either by email or through the US Postal Service, during the week prior to the service, a copy of the reading, prayers, or other liturgical acts in which he or she will serve. This is not to guarantee a good performance but to enable each person to offer the best of his or her God-given talents to ennoble the assembly's doxology.

Assemblies easily can detect whether the various elements of the service—including the sermon—blend harmoniously or, on the other hand, worshipers are being forced into a discordant maze of disconnected worship expressions thrown together before the church secretary leaves the office on a Friday afternoon. Don Saliers raises some fundamental questions instructive for all who craft and lead worship: preachers, presiders, musicians, artists, storytellers, ushers, greeters, and even parking-lot attendants:

> How may we find again, for our present circumstances, the sense of awe and mystery, the sense of delight and spontaneity, the sense of knowing and being known by God truthfully, and the sense of hope in a confusing and violent world?

8. Paul Scott Wilson, *Imagination of the Heart: New Understandings of Preaching* (Nashville: Abingdon, 1988), 86.

When we sing, "The hopes and fears of all the years are met in thee tonight," what hopes and fears do we bring? When, in Advent, we sing, "O come, O come, Emmanuel," what longings for our world and for our lives are made present? If we sing "Spirit of the living God, fall afresh on me," what do we expect? These questions point in the direction of a different kind of preparation, and a more attentive participation. Why do we settle for so little when God offers so much in Word, sacrament, and song?[9]

The late British Methodist minister and hymn-writer Fred Pratt Green in 1972 wrote a hymn in celebration of music in the worship. Although the images are related to music, in a larger sense "music" could be replaced by "liturgy," "preaching," and "worship."

When in our music God is glorified,
and adoration leaves no room for pride,
it is as though the whole creation cried
Alleluia!

How often, making music, we have found
a new dimension in the world of sound,
as worship moved us to a more profound
Alleluia!

So has the Church, in liturgy and song,
in faith and love, through centuries of wrong,
borne witness to the truth in every tongue,
Alleluia!

And did not Jesus sing a psalm that night
when utmost evil strove against the Light?
Then let us sing, for whom he won the fight,
Alleluia!

9. Saliers, *Worship Come to Its Senses*, 15.

Let every instrument be tuned for praise!
Let all rejoice who have a voice to raise!
And may God give us faith to sing always
Alleluia! Amen.[10]

The second stanza captures what happens when worship is offered doxologically "as worship moved [moves] us to a more profound Alleluia!" That phrase has inspired the title of a collection of essays on the relationship between theology and worship edited by Leanne Van Dyk. It was the phrase from Fred Pratt Green's hymn that enticed me to buy the book: *A More Profound Alleluia: Theology and Worship in Harmony*.[11] Each of the chapters is the juxtaposition of a theological treatise on an act in the worship *ordo*—from gathering to sending—with two hymns that the authors believe reflect the theological intention of each of the worship acts, parts of the service, that is. Van Dyk explains the connection in her introduction to the collection: "The deep integrations of theology and worship that have always found voice in the text and music of a first-rate hymn are being examined once again by liturgical theologians, systematic theologians, and pastors who want to engage their congregations in theologically coherent patterns of worship. What is being discovered anew are the many natural and nuanced ways that one's theology impacts one's worship and one's worship impacts one's theology."[12] During my theological training, Franz Hildebrandt at Drew University taught a course on the theology of John and Charles Wesley through a study of a collection of their hymns. Hymns—including those of the Wesleys—are not intended primarily as theological documents but as acts of an assembly's corporate doxologizing. Hymns are meant to be sung, and, as such, in Fred Pratt Green's words, they find "a new dimension of

10. Fred Pratt Green © 1972 by Hope Publishing Co., Carol Stream, IL 60188. All rights reserved. Used by permission.
11. Leanne Van Dyk, ed., *A More Profound Alleluia: Theology and Worship in Harmony* (Grand Rapids: Eerdmans, 2005).
12. Van Dyk, ed., *A More Profound Alleluia*, xvi.

sound," a new dimension of gospeling that moves an assembly to a more profound doxology.

Recently I participated in an evensong liturgy in which every expression in the *ordo* was sung. This was not a hymn-sing as is popular in some churches as a fill-in while the pastor is on vacation and in which those in the assembly yell out the numbers of hymns in the hymnal. Rather, the intention was carefully and artfully to craft the entire service as a sung liturgy employing hymns, chants, and canticles that were sung by the assembly and cantors. Even the sermon was a carefully juxtaposed series of congregational hymns that transposed the biblical texts of the day into psalms, hymns, and spiritual songs that preached the Word of God. The singing was accompanied by gifted musicians on piano, flute, and drums. The whole service preached doxologically profoundly. The poet Victor Hugo once said, "Music expresses that which cannot be said and on which it is impossible to be silent."

It was the nineteenth-century German composer Richard Wagner who popularized the musical concept of a leitmotif, a brief musical phrase to identify a certain character or theme that occurs repeatedly throughout the piece of music. A leitmotif is a "guiding motif" intended to connect all parts of composition in a harmonious whole. The same concept can be employed liturgically and homiletically to enable a certain metaphor or phrase to occur repeatedly in the various individual elements in the *ordo* to foster an organic whole. What Paul Wilson says specifically about a sermon may be expanded to the whole of the preaching event that occurs throughout the liturgy:

> In both music and dance a central theme will be introduced early, only hinting at what is to come. The same may be true for preaching. The congregation wants to know, almost from the outset, what this sermon or homily is about. However often the central idea is repeated in the course of the preaching, as a general rule it should appear early. Stated early it does not give away the plot, since it is not developed, but

merely stands as a kind of signpost indicating the direction
we are going. Similarly, it is a good general rule to touch on
it again at the end, as a reminder of where we have been.
While it will only be developed in the one place . . . it needs
to be mentioned a minimum of three times for us to hear it.[13]

African American preachers have mastered the art of the leitmotif: repeating a phrase, generally a few words of the biblical text,
several times throughout the sermon, often to mark points of
thematic transition. Sometimes the repetitions are followed by
pauses that begin to invite the assembly to join the preacher in
vocalizing the words of the leitmotif. More on that later.

The phrase, "no exclusions," was a metaphoric phrase that
served as a leitmotif in worship on the Fifth Sunday of Easter in
Year B. The lection was Acts 8:26–40, the account of the encounter between Philip and the Ethiopian eunuch. "What is to prevent *me* from being baptized?" the eunuch asks. The question
is rhetorical, and the answer is self-evident: there are no exclusions to sacramental grace, and without words of explanation,
according to Luke, Philip baptizes him. The sermon—titled by
the leitmotif, "No Exclusions!"—ended:

> Radical inclusivity is a threat to some people, to some
> churches. But to others it is freedom and the source of new
> life. Hopefully to all it is gospel, not because *we* decide so, but
> because it's *God's Word*: no exceptions, no exclusions. These
> are the sacraments, these are the holy things—baptism and
> eucharist—that initiate us and feed us. I ask the question
> of the guy in the chariot: What is there to prevent *anyone*
> from being baptized and being fed at this table and being
> immersed in God's mysteries? No exceptions. No exclusions.

Yet, there were connectors before and after and throughout
the sermon that reinforced the leitmotif. At the beginning of
the service the assembly sang and invoked: "Jesus, thou art all

13. Wilson, *Imagination of the Heart*, 134.

compassion, pure, unbounded love thou art, visit us with thy salvation, enter every troubling heart." The hymn that immediately preceded the sermon, "As We Gather at Your Table," included, in the final stanza, this prayer: "Gracious Spirit, help us summon other guests to share that feast where triumphant Love will welcome those who had been last and least. There no more will envy blind us nor will pride our peace destroy, as we join with saints and angels to repeat the sounding joy."[14] Word led to sacrament, and the eucharistic prayer included the following doxological anamnesis:

Minister: Jesus, Son of God, we lift our hearts
in thankful remembrance
of your reconciling love,
outpoured on the cross once and for all time.

All: **We praise you for your victory over the powers**
of evil and death,
assuring us that neither life nor death
nor anything in all creation
can separate us from the love of God. . . .[15]

In the distribution of the communion no one was excluded. *Everyone* is invited. What is to prevent *anyone* from receiving sacramental grace? Throughout the liturgy the homiletical leitmotif emerged in various shapes and expressions with the intention of creating a harmonious whole. After the service one person said to me, almost tearfully, "No exclusions! My wife is a _____ and is musical director in _____ Church, yet she is excluded from receiving communion because she was divorced." The leitmotif connected with him and went with him out through the church door.

---

14. Words: Carl P. Daw Jr. © 1989 by Hope Publishing Co., Carol Stream, IL 60188.

15. From F. Russell Mitman, *Immersed in the Splendor of God: Resources for Worship Renewal* (Cleveland: Pilgrim, 2005).

A great deal of dialogue has been taking place in Europe between Protestants and Roman Catholics after five hundred years of conflict, particularly in relationship to the presence of Christ in holy communion and the prohibitions associated with the reception of the elements. In preparation for a common commemoration of the Reformation in 2017 a treatise was prepared by Roman Catholic and Lutheran commissions titled *From Conflict to Communion*.[16] This document, together with the book *What Happens in Holy Communion* by Reformed theologian Michael Welker, who teaches systematic theology at the University of Heidelberg, provide a healthy perspective on where ecumenical conversations are headed. Welker commented in 2000: "The ecumenical conversations of recent decades have been able to elucidate the rich and complex process of holy communion better than was possible in time of emphatic confessional controversies. In this way these ecumenical conversations represent contributions to ecumenical peace and are a particular blessing of the twentieth century."[17] The pain expressed by the person exiting the church cited above has been felt by many of us, and the official "fences" around the Lord's table that history erected are being breached unofficially by clergy and laypersons as reflected in the commentary of a ninety-two-year-old: "Jesus invites all; it's his table." Welker reminds: "The first recipients of Jesus' Supper: Judas who betrayed him, Peter who denied him, the disciples who abandoned him."[18]

Charles Jennens was the librettist for Handel's oratorio, *Messiah*. Jennens artfully juxtaposed biblical texts—many from the Old Testament—to invite the hearers themselves gradually to arrive at the affirmation: "Yes, Jesus is Messiah." Handel's artistry was to transpose those few sentences from the Bible into a profound doxology. Often the musical device that Handel used to heighten the intrinsic emotion of the texts was

16. *From Conflict to Communion: Lutheran-Catholic Common Commemoration of the Reformation in 2017* (Leipzig: Evangelische Verlagsanstalt, 2013).

17. Michael Welker, *What Happens in Holy Communion*, trans. John F. Hoffmeyer (Grand Rapids: Eerdmans, 2000), 23.

18. Welker, *What Happens in Holy Communion*, 71.

repetition. For example, in the opening chorus the choir sings: first by the altos: "And the glory, the glory of the Lord" followed by the basses repeating the same musical theme, "And the glory, the glory of the Lord" while sopranos and tenors sing the same words in a musical counterpoint. Then the tenors continue the phrase "shall be revealed, shall be revealed" with the basses, followed by sopranos, followed by the altos singing the same phrase as a fugue. Then the chorus in ensemble sings the entire phrase, "and the glory, the glory of the Lord shall be revealed." After a short musical interlude the altos begin the next phrase, "and all flesh shall see it together," followed by the tenors singing the same words and music. Then the last phrase, "for the mouth of the Lord hath spoken it" is introduced in unison by the men's voices followed by embellishments sung by the women's voices. Once the entire text has been introduced the choir juxtaposes the phrases that lead—after three quarter rests of pure silence—to the final adagio doxology, "hath spoken it." One-sentence—twenty-six words—of Isaiah 40:5 in constant repetition textually and musically is transposed, through the homiletical media of choir and orchestra in the context of a gathering of people with ears eager to hear, into a moment of doxology. When *Messiah* is sung by a choir and accompanied by musical instruments, the boundaries between "auditorium" and sacred space get blurred, and those who sing and play instruments in the presence of an assembly discover that together they have been immersed doxologically in the splendor of God.

There is a significant difference between intentional repetition and the senseless redundancy in some so-called "praise hymns." Recently an assembly of nearly three hundred souls was subjected to the same "I love Jesus" sung by a choir over and over at a deafening volume that I no longer had ears to hear, turning what was intended to be a doxology into a performance focused on the singers and their ability to shout as loud as possible. Although the assembly was invited to stand and sing along, I noticed that after about ten minutes the excess of sound exhausted the assembly; they stopped singing and sat down. The initial repetitions that had engaged the assembly eventuated in a theological and musical redundancy that became almost intolerable.

Rests are essential in music, and rests are necessary liturgically and homiletically. Television has conditioned viewers to assume that silence is indicative that something has gone wrong technologically or the speaker has become incapacitated. Radio disc-jockeys merge one song into the next without a pause. Silence is difficult for some people to cope with individually, and purposeful and liturgical silence in worship in most assemblies is either nonexistent or restricted to no longer than fifteen seconds. Liturgical rests are sacramental moments that can lead into individual and corporate immersion in God's splendor. Yes, rests provide for personal reflection and prayer, but purposeful rests also provide for an assembly's doxological silence, which spiritually may be more important than a lot of noisy gongs and clanging cymbals.

Likewise, homiletical rests are important in sermons. Artful and purposeful pauses in sermons are not just "stops" but moments of silence that allow for transition in the sermon's flow. Unlike a lecture in which the speaker says, "My second point is . . . ," a pause in a sermon is like a musical rest that is inherent in the music itself and moves the music to what will follow in the piece. I can remember a sermon—and I have no recollection of what the preacher said—in which the assembly was subjected to about forty minutes of rapid-fire words that seemed to have been shot from a homiletical machine gun. There were no rests in this barrage, and what was intended to be communicated was lost in all the verbiage. Preachers and assemblies need purposeful rests to allow the Word of God to penetrate through walls of words.

Incidentally, the "By the way's" that find their way into most of my sermons are, I believe, "verbal sidebars" that provide for brief educational moments, short humorous or ironic interjections, and even some one-sentence personal commentaries. These verbal sidebars provide the assembly with "breathers" along the way through the sermon. However, care needs to be taken that sidebars do not become sidetracks that lead the assembly off the main trajectory of the homiletical event.

Preaching doxologically therefore involves being sensitive to tempo and dynamics both in the sermon itself and in its setting within the whole liturgy. Composers of music often suggest tempos at which they desire their compositions to be performed. Conductors, soloists, and instrumentalists have a certain liberty of tempos and dynamics, yet that freedom of performance must lie within the parameters established by the composers. The Scriptures themselves often dictate the tempo and dynamics of liturgy and sermon. For example, in the passion narrative the repeated shout "Crucify him!" needs to be articulated as though it is coming from a crowd. Usually, I print that portion of the gospel narrative, and the whole assembly is urged to shout "Crucify him!" in response to Pilate's question, "Then what shall I do with this man you call the king of the Jews?" (Mark 15:12). Likewise, the Easter acclamation, "The Lord is risen! He is risen indeed!" wants shouts accompanied by trumpets, bells, drums, and any other instruments that can produce a joyful noise. I once presided in an assembly on Easter, and the opening hymn was sung so slowly that every syllable seemed to have a hyphen placed after it. I wondered if the folks really believed that "Christ the Lord is risen today!" I also have endured sermons in which the preacher seemed to want to ar-tic-u-late ev-er-y syl-la-ble, and I wanted to yell out, "Get real!" There's a homiletical middle ground between being chatty and pompous, between intimate and bellicose. The word of God deserves a more profound doxology.

It may seem a strange question to ask: "Does your church preach doxologically?" I mean, does the architecture praise *God* inside and outside? Does the building and do the appointments inside and outside invite people into the mystery of God? Does the church proclaim the word of God in art and symbols that offer to God and to the people of God a more profound doxology than words can convey?

Most travelers are awed by the splendor of gothic and renaissance cathedrals of Europe, but there are still a few ethical

pragmatists who ask the Judas question, "Why wasn't this per-
fume sold and the money given to the poor?" (John 12:5 NIV)
or the parish ethicist's question, "With so much poverty all
around the church, why is more and more money being spent
on keeping up the building?" Judas raised the question out of
criminal intent. Even the ethical question misses the doxological intent—the building is intended to glorify God and to invite
people into the mystery of what happens in that sacred space.
The sight of a twelfth-century cathedral rising with the morning sun on a hilltop in Tuscany beckons the traveler today as
it did to pilgrims in days long before buses filled with tourists:
"Come, all who are weary and heavy laden." The western façade
of Notre Dame cathedral in Paris, glowing in late-afternoon
sunlight, preaches the gospel in its ancient gothic stonework
and invites even the casual onlooker to go inside and be immersed in the cosmic mystery. I admit that the intention of the
builders of and contributors to many great Christian churches
was to demonstrate political and economic power. Yet, their
legacies, centuries later, transcend the principalities and powers of architects and benefactors to show to all who have eyes
to see, ears to hear, and feet to walk or wheels to roll inside,
truly profound doxologies.

Many great churches throughout the world contain, intrin-
sically within their design or through later renovation and ad-
dition, great artistic creations that were intended to preach the
gospel and to enable assemblies to offer to God profound doxologies. The liturgical and homiletical symbols of artistically
crafted pulpits, fonts/baptisteries, lecterns, altars/tables were
more than functional pieces of ecclesiastical furniture. They
were, in the various centuries in which they were fashioned,
and still are, intrinsic accompaniments to Word and Sacrament.
Stained glass preaches the biblical story, and when medieval
glass became the victim of war, contemporary windows, such
as Marc Chagall's nine luminous blue windows in the cathedral
in Mainz, Germany, were installed in gothic window frames.
Following the Luftwaffe's firebombing of Coventry, England,
the fourteenth-century Cathedral of St. Michael was left in

smoldering ruins. The new cathedral, constructed next to the bombed-out ruins and dedicated in 1962, has as its focal point a giant tapestry by Graham Sutherland above the altar drawing the human eye into the mystery of the resurrected Christ. Great art is doxological. Yet, no art is better than bad art. Too many churches in the 1970s tried to brighten up their worship spaces with felt banners constructed by kids in vacation Bible school. Today, perhaps as they were when first hung on drapery rods, they are more distractions than windows into transcendent realities.

Church architecture preaches. Robert Webber commented:

> In the beauty of the temple [in ancient Israel] God keeps before his people the vision of the new heavens and new earth. Historic Christian churches have also kept God's vision alive in their worship space. Unfortunately the modern and contemporary church has, for the most part, disregarded God's cosmic vision and has reduced space to a utilitarian usage. Now that we live in a more visual period of history, younger leaders in particular are rediscovering how space speaks and are looking once again to the rediscovery of biblical and historical worship.[19]

Of course, cruciform cathedrals present many architectural challenges for doing today's liturgy and preaching. The same is true for most Protestant meeting houses designed for assemblies to remain seated in tidy rows of pews bolted to the floor. Then there are the postmodern movie-house-inspired auditoriums—one such establishment calls itself the "movie church" because it began in a cinema and later built a vinyl-clad, virtually windowless structure, even with a cinematic marquee. I have spent many hours consulting with churches on ways to adapt their legacy spaces for doing today's liturgy and preaching. One astute layperson in a church in dire need

19. Robert E. Webber, *Ancient-Future Worship: Proclaiming and Enacting God's Narrative* (Grand Rapids: Baker, 2008), 65.

of renovation fifty or so years after its construction remarked: "This church was an architect's dream, a builder's challenge, and the congregation's nightmare." Most often the original intention of adaptive reuse is functionality, that is, to redo a space within certain budget restraints, to meet an assembly's immediate needs for accessibility, acoustics, lighting, comfort, and ability for the assembly to move in rhythm with the liturgy. Yet, my hope is that in such redoings congregations, without resorting to fake stone and carpeted concrete, can fashion sacred spaces that truly gospel the Christian faith doxologically and enable assemblies within those sanctified spaces to offer a more profound doxology.

Johann Sebastian Bach penned at the end of his works the three letters "S. D. G.," an abbreviation for the ancient but simple doxology: "Soli Deo Gloria" ("Glory to God alone"). The intention of "S. D. G." was to proclaim that the particular composition was created solely for the praise of God and not for performers or audiences or even the patrons and patronesses who employed him. Many of Bach's pieces where intended primarily for liturgical settings, as transpositions of hymns, words of the mass, and biblical passages into magnificent doxologies "to the glory of God alone." It is worthy of emulation for the crafting of any liturgy and any sermon to begin, continue, and end with "S. D. G." to invite any assembly into a more profound doxology.

11

*Preaching **Eschatologically***

Long ago God spoke to our ancestors in many and various ways
by the prophets, but in these last days he has spoken to us by a
Son, whom he appointed heir of all things, through whom he
also created the worlds. He is the reflection of God's glory and
the exact imprint of God's very being, and he sustains all things
by his powerful word.

—Hebrews 1:1–3

"I am the Alpha and the Omega, the first and the last, the
beginning and the end."

—Revelation 12:13

It can be assumed that preaching eschatologically should
be the last thing considered as the last chapter of these reflections. "Eschatology," from the Greek *eschatos* ("last"), com-
pounded with *logia* ("study" or "knowledge"), generally is associated with the theological study of "last things," or "end-time."
To some preachers eschatology is deemed a kind of appendix
that can be skipped while to others of an opposite bent, it is
the core of their theology and preaching.

David Prince, in his blog "Prince on Preaching," posts: "We
live and preach in the same age as the apostles, the already-
but-not-yet of the kingdom of Christ. . . . Every faithful sermon

is eschatological because in Jesus, the end has begun. The eschatological cruciform community of the church serves and proclaims the Gospel in the tension of living in the overlap of the ages. . . . Faithful preaching is not only eschatologically oriented; it is itself an eschatological event" (March 4, 2014). Although I do not find myself in agreement with Prince in what he says in the part of the quotation represented here by ellipses, it is his final conclusion that caught my eye: "Faithful preaching is not only eschatologically oriented, it is itself an eschatological event." Much has been said and written about "eschatological preaching," yet to entertain the idea that preaching is itself eschatologically oriented and itself an eschatological *event* pushes "eschatology" into the adverbial: *eschatologically*. Preaching eschatologically is enabling an assembly to participate in the already-but-not-yet-ness of the word of God that I introduced in chapter 4.

In my study of the Greek text of Hebrews 1:1–4 (appointed as Proper 22 between October 2 and October 8 in Year B of the Revised Common Lectionary), I stumbled across *eschatos* in the first sentence, *ep' eschatou tōn hymerōn toutōn*, "in these last days. . . ." "Long ago God spoke to our ancestors in many and various ways by the prophets, but *in these last days* he has spoken to us by a Son, whom he appointed heir of all things, through whom he also created the worlds." The writer to the Hebrews affirms that the eschatological event *already* has happened through God's Son whom God appointed "heir of all things" and through whom all of creation came into being ("In the beginning was the Word, and the Word was with God and the Word was God . . ."—John 1:1). The "last," *eschaton*, already is present reality through the birth, death, resurrection, and ascension of Christ. To preach eschatologically is to invite an assembly homiletically and liturgically into the "last" that already is in Christ. Word and Sacrament are eschatological happenings *now* in "*these* days." A beloved college professor of mine was asked by a door-to-door religious pamphleteer, "Are you ready?" "Ready for what?" Charlie responded, tongue-in-cheek. "Why, for the second coming!"

Charlie: "Was there ever a *first*?" The guy with his pamphlets walked silently away.

Yet, we need to be reminded that *eschatos* is also an adjective relating to the future, to the not-yet-ness of God. The late Robert Webber wrote in his last book, which was published posthumously: "I was in seminary during the middle of the twentieth century. At that time *eschatology* meant the charting out of the end-time events, the rapture, the second coming, the battle of Armageddon, and all the issues that cluster around what are called *the last days*. There certainly is a continued interest in these matters, as shown by the popularity of the *Left Behind* series and the current political issues centering around the Middle East."[1] Webber was schooled in such a perspective, yet he evolved, through his study of the ancient Christian writings, into an ecumenical theologian and liturgiologist who produced, beginning in 1999, the *Ancient Future* series and developed a following among what came to be called "postmoderns" and the "emerging church" movement. His final book on ancient future worship includes the chapter "Worship *Anticipates* the Future," in which he says, "God has a future for his world. Therefore, the whole story of God is not contained completely in past events. . . . God is working in past and present events to bring about this future. . . . The eschatological nature of worship is more than preaching a sermon on future events. The content of eschatological worship has to do with God's rescue of the entire created order . . . when God's rule is being done *on earth as it is in heaven.*"[2] Webber's journey is a helpful paradigm for those of us who did not begin where he did and even for those of us who simply avoided eschatological texts in Bible and tradition or deconstructed them to fit them into narrowed frames of looking at reality, particularly, when individualized, regarding what happens or does not happen after death. Popular culture, even among those who claim to be religious, has invented eschato-

---

1. Robert E. Webber, *Ancient-Future Worship: Proclaiming and Enacting God's Narrative* (Grand Rapids: Baker, 2008), 57.

2. Webber, *Ancient-Future Worship*, 57–58.

logical platitudes supposedly to soothe the blow of mortality. Yet they have little to do with the affirmation, as encapsulated in the church's ancient creed of Nicea: "We look for the resurrection of the dead, and the life of the world to come."

When I was a judicatory minister, I proposed that every candidate for ordination write a funeral sermon. The idea seemed rather radical to some, yet the practice continues today. For the preparation of a sermon for a funeral will force the preacher to focus on what is the core of the Christian faith: the resurrection of Jesus Christ and what we—the church—look for in the "resurrection of the dead and the life of the world to come." Preachers wrestling with the reality of resurrection will be redirected from the idea that a funeral sermon is a eulogy extolling the virtues of the deceased to what it means to be "buried with Christ in baptism into death, so that, just as Christ was raised from the dead by the glory of the Father, so we too might walk in newness of life" (Rom. 6:4). Let the eulogizing be appointed to a very few family or friends, and preach the resurrection and what it means to live and die in Christ.

Preaching a funeral sermon centered in the resurrection is but a part of a whole homiletical and liturgical event that invites all assembled into the eschatological reality of Jesus's promise, "Where I am there you shall be also" (John)—not only *after* death but also happening *now*. The future impinges on the present in Word and Sacrament. Many years ago it came to me that eucharist in a funeral service is not "too Catholic" and should not be restricted to those whose profession is through Rome. I have found a receptivity to including eucharist far beyond my imagination. Recently there was a funeral service for a beloved member of the congregation I serve. The church was filled mostly with those who were not a part of that denominational family. I was astounded that when the invitation was announced, "Come, for all things are ready," probably 80 to 90 percent of the assembly came forward, without being ushered, to receive the bread and wine. It appeared that so many wanted to *do* in the eucharist what they had just affirmed in the creed: "I believe in the . . . communion of saints, the forgiveness of sins, and the life everlasting." That assembly truly was engaged eschatologically in realities not bounded by time and space and ecclesiastic restrictions. When I shared this story with a friend, he responded, "Often the laypeople are far ahead of church officials."

Don Saliers devotes an entire chapter in *Worship as Theology* to "The Eschatological Character of Worship." He writes:

> The realized eschatology embedded in the liturgical action of the community at prayer in Jesus' name is not simply a recall of the "fact" of a resurrection in the past. Rather it bespeaks and enacts the impossible possibility of the future becoming present. The present outpouring of the Spirit that brings all things to memory about the whole history of God's passion for the suffering, groaning creation, is a crisis in time, for the Spirit enables us to remember what has not yet come to be in history. Here we dare, even in our not comprehending, to join in the ending cry that is our beginning, "Maranatha!"
> . . . The eschaton is God-given, literally not conceivable in human schemes. Not a date, but a promised faithfulness. Not something guaranteed by proper liturgy, but a radical risk of faith.[3]

Preaching eschatologically is inviting the assembly into the open-ended-ness of the gospel and, on the human side, "a radical risk of faith." To tie the sermon up in concluding "therefores" is really idolatrous. Human words are not adequate to say what God will do when the preacher stops talking. Perhaps just an open-ended stop may be a better invitation into God's mystery.

Apparently I have become known in the town in which I serve as the preacher "who just stops." Here is a closing excerpt from a sermon for a community Lenten service in which I was asked to preach on 1 Corinthians 2:1–2—"When I came to you, brothers and sisters, I did not come proclaiming the mystery

---

3. Don E. Saliers, *Worship as Theology: Foretaste of Glory Divine* (Nashville: Abingdon, 1994), 68.

of God to you in lofty words or wisdom. For I decided to know nothing among you except Jesus Christ, and him crucified."

I know that I am preaching to the choir tonight and that because we are here tonight together across Phoenixville's ecumenical spectrum, a privatized spirituality for us here obviously is not enough. And there are others who find themselves in our churches because a privatized spirituality is not enough to get them through the wildernesses of life's crises. They want to experience among your assemblies the mystery of God, they want to get to know nothing else but Christ crucified, no religious travelogues to faraway places with strange-sounding names, no group therapy sessions, no political campaign speeches, and they turn to you—all of you, clergy and religious and lay alike—they turn to you and me and ask as those Greeks asked the apostle Philip, "Sir, ma'am, we wish to see Jesus." They want to come to know Christ crucified. Only in communion with other pilgrims in this spiritually barren land will they and you discover that instead of *us* seeking God, *God* finds us. That's the mystery: in trying to find God, God finds us. You may not be confronted by a blinding light like Paul, but you may find yourself knocked off your hobby horse, and all you can say to the mystery is, "Oh, my God! My God!"

Preaching eschatologically is allowing God to finish the sermon and leaving it up to God to add an "amen," if and when God so decides.

Every consideration of things eschatological is confronted by words in the last chapter of the Bible, "I am the Alpha and the Omega, the first [*prōtos* in Greek] and the last [*eschatos*], the beginning [*archē*] and the end [*telos*]" (Rev. 22:13). The "I am" is, to John of Patmos, the risen and ascended Christ encompassing the whole of the Trinitarian Godhead—creation to consummation. So, first things are seen through the lens of last things, and endings through beginnings. Yet, "end" is not "cessation" or "termination" but "goal," as that to which reality is moving, literally from the Greek *telos*, "far off," hence the word "teleological," and everyday things like "telescope," "telephone," and "television."

In the book of Hebrews Christ is both the "starter" and the "finisher" of our faith: "Therefore, since we are surrounded by so great a cloud of witnesses, let us also lay aside every weight and the sin that clings so closely, and let us run with perseverance the race that is set before us, looking to Jesus, the *archēgos* and *teleiōtēs* of our faith" (Heb. 12:1–2). The athletic imagery of the "race that is set before us" can obscure the eschatological dimensions of this text. The focus is not on the runner—and all the allegorical images preachers can wring out of that—but on *Christ* who marks the beginning of faith and is at the consummation of faith. Hence, symbolically faith begins at the font and ends at the font. All worship and preaching begins at the font and ends at the font, where Christ is as "*archēgos* and *teleiōtēs* of our faith," "alpha and omega," "*prōtos* and *eschatos*."

It is also easy to miss the eschatology in Charles Wesley's hymn, "Love Divine, All Loves Excelling" (1747), an allusion to 1 Corinthians 13:13, "but the greatest of these is love." Despite the arguments over the centuries regarding Wesley's "perfectionist" ideas in the original "second rest" and "take away the power of sinning" phrases, the eschatology in the second stanza is unescapable: "Alpha and omega be; end of faith as its beginning, set our hearts at liberty," and in the fourth stanza, "Finish, then, thy new creation, pure and spotless let us be . . . till we cast our crowns before thee, lost in wonder, love, and praise." The hymn is a prayer to Christ who, in Wesley's words, is "pure, unbounded love." This hymn is but one example of many great hymns of the faith that immerse the singers in the eschatological mystery. The subtitle of Don Saliers's *Worship as Theology* is *Foretaste of Glory Divine*, from the opening stanza of Fanny Crosby's (1873) gospel hymn, "Blessed assurance, Jesus is mine! Oh, what a foretaste of glory divine . . ."

Preaching eschatologically in North America is difficult in the season of Advent. The church year ends with the Festival of Christ the King (Reign of Christ), which generally falls on a Sunday at the end of November and is sometimes coincidental with the four-day national Thanksgiving Day holiday weekend. Sometimes, the First Sunday in Advent also falls on the weekend preceded by Thanksgiving Day on Thursday and "Black Friday," when the commercial countdown to Christmas officially begins. (Most stores already have changed merchandise from Halloween goblins to Santas by the 31st of October!) All Saints Day (November 1) never made it into most Protestant calendars in the USA. By then the race to Christmas is on, and celebrating Advent is relegated to lighting an additional candle on each of the four Sundays prior to Christmas. But, by the Fourth Sunday, Advent generally has been totally eclipsed by children's pageants and choir cantatas. Despite the best intentions of some church leaders to keep Advent in Advent, the push to celebrate culture's Christmas in Advent often overrides best intentions.

The "He comes" texts, both biblical and liturgical, are rich in eschatological expectation of what God will do in God's future—always a "not-yet-ness" of God's "already-ness." Yet, in much of church life the advent of God's coming in judgment and grace has been replaced by birth-of-a-baby niceties, and in some quarters, Advent's traditional purple of preparation for a royal arrival has been replaced by Mary's baby-blue vestments. Churches have difficulty with Advent's eschatological paradox: Christ *is coming*, yet Christ *has come*. There was a "first" coming, and it's hard to get to the idea that Christ *will come again*, even though we say it in the eucharistic acclamation and we hope and pray all the time that Christ's kingdom will come and God's will *will be done* on earth as it is in heaven, even *now*. In his final chapter, "Advent and Eschaton," Don Saliers says, "We must think *from* the future toward the present in light of the past. . . . The church's liturgy in some way is always Advent, is always '*Maranatha!*,' hovering between 'Come, Lord!' and 'The Lord is come!' This points toward that which is yet to be, but which must be continuous with what we know of

God's self-giving."[4] Preaching eschatologically is inviting an assembly liturgically and homiletically into the Advent paradox of God's "already-but-not-yet-ness" for the living of *these* days. Preaching Christ is enticing an assembly liturgically and homiletically to enter into the eschatological mystery. And that, almost ironically, is what we are told younger generations than ours are looking for—a mystery greater than themselves.

Frank Senn, in the next-to-the-last page of his extensive (755 pages) *Christian Liturgy: Catholic and Evangelical*, writes:

> The eschatological vision may sometimes be dim inside the church, but the sense of the eschaton is entirely missing outside the church. . . . Liturgy in this postmodern world must aim for enchantment, not entertainment. Entertainment is a major facet of our culture. But entertainment as a cultural model is inadequate to the mission of the gospel because it works best when it leaves one satisfied with oneself and one's world. Enchantment, on the other hand, casts a spell that leads one from a drab world to another, brighter, more interesting world.[5]

*   *   *

In more than a half-century I have attempted liturgically and homiletically to invite individuals and assemblies into the brighter, more interesting world of the gospel. In this volume I have attempted to provide in some broad brushstrokes the art of preaching adverbially that I have gleaned from others and from my own experience in the homiletical and liturgical arts. Some of the shapers on my journey have been professors and teachers. Some have been colleagues in ministry. Some have been the faithful who defy culture's Sunday lurings and

4. Saliers, *Worship as Theology*, 229.
5. Frank C. Senn, *Christian Liturgy: Catholic and Evangelical* (Minneapolis: Fortress, 1997), 704.

dare to step over the churches' doorsills. And, of course, some are those whose witness to the Word inscribed words that became the Bible and that may, through the Holy Spirit, become the Word of God for the living of these days. I offer these reflections that hopefully they may benefit the church's leaders and assemblies yet to emerge through the wonder workings of the triune God.

SOLI DEO GLORIA.

Select Bibliography

Author's Note: This bibliography is a sampling of books and articles that have helped shape my understandings of the homiletical and liturgical disciplines involved in an integrated approach to Christian worship. Some are classics that are shelved in libraries and deserve to be reexplored. Others remain in print or are available in reissued editions. Still others are recent publications with new insights on what happens when assemblies find themselves in an encounter with the living Word of God.

Abba, Raymond. *Principles of Christian Worship.* London: Oxford University Press, 1957.

Anderson, Scott. "Context, Margins, and Ministry: A Church in the Pacific Northwest's 'None Zone.'" In *Worship and Culture: Foreign Country or Homeland?*, ed. Gláucia Vasconcelos Wilkey, 84–106. Grand Rapids: Eerdmans, 2014.

Andreopoulos, Andreas. *The Sign of the Cross: The Gesture, the Mystery, the History.* Brewster, MA: Paraclete, 2006.

Baptism, Eucharist and Ministry. Faith and Order Paper No. 111. Geneva: World Council of Churches, 1982.

Barrett, Lee C., trans. *The Heidelberg Catechism: A New Translation for the 21st Century.* Cleveland: Pilgrim, 2007.

Barth, Karl. *The Word of God and the Word of Man.* Translated by Douglas Horton. New York: Harper & Brothers, 1956.

Berger, Teresa, and Bryan D. Spinks. *The Spirit in Worship—Worship in the Spirit.* Collegeville, MN: Liturgical Press, 2009.

Bonhoeffer, Dietrich. *Worldly Preaching: Lectures on Homiletics.* Edited and translated by Clyde E. Fant. New York: Thomas Nelson, 1975.

Borchert, Gerald L. *Worship in the New Testament: Divine Mystery and Human Response.* St. Louis: Chalice, 2008.

Brueggemann, Walter. *Finally Comes the Poet: Daring Speech for Proclamation.* Minneapolis: Augsburg Fortress, 1989.

_____. *Texts under Negotiation: The Bible and Postmodern Imagination.* Minneapolis: Augsburg Fortress, 1993.

_____. *The Prophetic Imagination.* Philadelphia: Fortress, 1978.

Burgess, John P. *Why Scripture Matters: Reading the Bible in a Time of Church Conflict.* Louisville: Westminster John Knox, 1998.

Christopherson, D. Foy. *A Place of Encounter: Renewing Worship Spaces.* Minneapolis: Augsburg Fortress, 2004.

Clark, Timothy. "The Function and Task of Liturgical Preaching." *St. Vladimir's Theological Quarterly* 45, no. 1 (2001): 25–54.

Craddock, Fred B. *As One without Authority*, rev. ed. St. Louis: Chalice, 2004.

_____. *Overhearing the Gospel: Preaching and Teaching the Faith to Persons Who Have Heard It All Before.* Nashville: Abingdon, 1992.

_____. *Preaching.* Nashville: Abingdon, 1985.

Cullmann, Oscar. *Early Christian Worship.* Translated by A. Stewart Todd and James B. Torrance. London: SCM, 1953.

Daniel, Lillian. *When "Spiritual But Not Religious" Is Not Enough.* New York: Jericho Books, 2013.

Davis, Ellen F. *Preaching the Luminous Word: Biblical Sermons and Homiletical Essays.* Grand Rapids: Eerdmans, 2016.

Dawn, Marva J. *Keeping the Sabbath Wholly.* Grand Rapids: Eerdmans, 1989.

_____. *Powers, Weakness, and the Tabernacling of God.* Grand Rapids: Eerdmans, 2001.

_____. *Reaching Out without Dumbing Down: A Theology of Worship for the Turn-of-the-Century Culture.* Grand Rapids: Eerdmans, 1995.

_____. *A Royal "Waste" of Time: The Splendor of Worshiping God and Being Church for the World.* Grand Rapids: Eerdmans, 1999.

Dix, Dom Gregory. *The Shape of the Liturgy.* London: A. C. Black, 1945.

Doran, Carol, and Thomas H. Troeger. *Trouble at the Table: Gathering the Tribes for Worship.* Nashville: Abingdon, 1992.

Driscoll, Jeremy, OSB. "Catechesis and Doctrine in Liturgical Preaching," 2013 USCCB Conference on "Preaching the Mystery of Faith," October 1, 2013.

Ebeling, Gerhard. *Word and Faith*. Translated by James W. Leitch. Philadelphia: Fortress, 1963.

Edgerton, W. Dow. *The Passion of Interpretation*. Louisville: Westminster John Knox, 1992.

Egge, Mandus A., ed. *Worship: Good News in Action*. Minneapolis: Augsburg, 1973.

Franke, Friedrich, ed. *Dr. Martin Luther's sämtliche Schriften*, vol. 11: *Die Evangelienpredigten*. Leipzig: E. Schimmel, 1846.

Frankforter, A. Daniel. *Stones for Bread: A Critique of Contemporary Worship*. Louisville: Westminster John Knox, 2001.

From Conflict to Communion: Lutheran-Catholic Common Commemoration of the Reformation in 2017. Leipzig: Evangelische Verlagsanstalt, 2013; new edition: Grand Rapids: Eerdmans, 2017.

Galbreath, Paul. *Leading from the Table*. The Alban Institute, 2008.

Galli, Mark. "*Speak* the Gospel: Use Deeds When Necessary." *The Christian Century*, May 21, 2009.

Giere, Samuel. "Preaching as Sacrament of the Word." Blog: Monday, January 5, 2009.

Hageman, Howard G. *Pulpit and Table: Some Chapters in the History of Worship in the Reformed Churches*. Richmond, VA: John Knox, 1962.

Hardin, H. Grady. *The Leadership of Worship*. Nashville: Abingdon, 1980.

Hardin, H. Grady, Joseph D. Quillian Jr., and James F. White. *The Celebration of the Gospel*. Nashville: Abingdon, 1964, 1980.

Hauerwas, Stanley. *Unleashing the Scripture: Freeing the Bible from Captivity to America*. Nashville: Abingdon, 1993.

Herberg, Will, ed. *Community, State, and Church: Three Essays by Karl Barth*. Translated by G. Ronald Howe. Garden City, NY: Anchor/Doubleday, 1960.

Hjelm, Norman A. "From the Past to the Future: The LWF Study Series on Worship and Culture as Vision and Mission." In *Worship and Culture: Foreign Country or Homeland?*, ed. Gláucia Vasconcelos Wilkey, 2–9. Grand Rapids: Eerdmans, 2014.

Hoon, Paul Waltman. *The Integrity of Worship: Ecumenical and Pastoral Studies in Liturgical Theology*. Nashville: Abingdon, 1971.

Hughes, Robert G., and Robert Kysar. *Preaching Doctrine for the Twenty-First Century*. Minneapolis: Fortress, 1997.

Irwin, Kevin W. *Responses to 101 Questions on the Mass*. Mahwah, NJ: Paulist Press, 1999.

Jensen, Richard A. *Envisioning the Word: The Use of Visual Image in Preaching*. Minneapolis: Augsburg Fortress, 2005.

Kelsey, Morton T. *Healing and Christianity*. New York: Harper & Row, 1976.

Kümmel, Werner Georg. *Promise and Fulfillment: The Eschatological Message of Jesus*. Translated by Dorothea M. Barton. London: SCM, 1957.

Lang, Dirk G. "Worship: Translating the Untranslatable." In *Worship and Culture: Foreign Country or Homeland?*, ed. Gláucia Vasconcelos Wilkey, 162–81. Grand Rapids: Eerdmans, 2014.

Lathrop, Gordon W. *Central Things: Worship in Word and Sacrament*. Minneapolis: Augsburg Fortress, 2005.

_____. "Every Foreign Country a Homeland, Every Homeland a Foreign Country: On Worship and Culture." In *Worship and Culture: Foreign Country or Homeland?*, ed. Gláucia Vasconcelos Wilkey, 10–34. Grand Rapids: Eerdmans, 2014.

_____. *Holy Ground: A Liturgical Cosmology*. Minneapolis: Augsburg Fortress, 2003.

_____. *Holy People: A Liturgical Ecclesiology*. Minneapolis: Augsburg Fortress, 1999.

_____. *Holy Things: A Liturgical Theology*. Minneapolis: Augsburg Fortress, 1993.

_____, ed. *Open Questions in Christian Worship*. Minneapolis: Augsburg Fortress, 1995.

Long, Kimberly Bracken. *The Worshiping Body: The Art of Leading Worship*. Louisville: Westminster John Knox, 2009.

Long, Thomas G. "And How Shall They Hear? The Listener in Contemporary Preaching." In *Listening to the Word: Studies in Honor of Fred B. Craddock*, ed. R. O'Day and Thomas G. Long, 167–88. Nashville: Abingdon, 1993.

_____. *Beyond the Worship Wars: Building Vital and Faithful Worship*. The Alban Institute, 2001.

_____. *Preaching and the Literary Forms of the Bible*. Philadelphia: Fortress, 1989.

Lowry, Eugene L. "The Revolution of Sermonic Shape." In *Listening to the Word: Studies in Honor of Fred B. Craddock*, ed. Gail R. O'Day and Thomas G. Long, 93–112. Nashville: Abingdon, 1993.

Macleod, Donald. "The Integrity of Preaching." In *Word and Sacrament: A Preface to Preaching and Worship*, 3–15. Englewood Cliffs, NJ: Prentice-Hall, 1960.

McEntyre, Marilyn. "Letting Words Do Their Work." *Christianity Today*, September 22, 2009.

Miller, Barbara Day. *Encounters with the Holy*. The Alban Institute, 2010.

Mitman, F. Russell. *Blessed by the Presence of God: Liturgies for Occasional Services*. Cleveland: Pilgrim, 2007.

_____. "Fifty Years of Worship in the United Church of Christ." In *Prism: A Theological Forum for the United Church of Christ* 21, no. 1 (Spring 2007): 33–46.

_____. *Immersed in the Splendor of God: Resources for Worship Renewal*. Cleveland: Pilgrim, 2005.

_____. *Worship in the Shape of Scripture*. Cleveland: Pilgrim, 2001, 2nd ed. 2009.

Moore-Keish, Martha L. *Do This in Remembrance of Me: A Ritual Approach to Reformed Eucharistic Theology*. Grand Rapids: Eerdmans, 2008.

Nevin, John W. *The Mystical Presence: A Vindication of the Reformed or Calvinistic Doctrine of the Holy Eucharist*. Philadelphia: J. B. Lippincott & Co., 1846.

Nichols, James Hastings. *Corporate Worship in the Reformed Tradition*. Philadelphia: Westminster, 1968.

_____. "The Reformed Doctrine of the Lord's Supper Recovered," "Baptismal Grace," and "The New Liturgy." In *Romanticism in American Theology: Nevin and Schaff at Mercersburg*, 24–106, 236–58, 281–307. Chicago: University of Chicago Press, 1961.

O'Day, Gail R. "Toward a Biblical Theology of Preaching." In *Listening to the Word: Studies in Honor of Fred B. Craddock*, ed. Gail R. O'Day and Thomas G. Long, 17–32. Nashville: Abingdon, 1993.

Ong, Walter J. *Orality and Literacy: The Technologizing of the Word*. London: Routledge, 1993.

Ott, Heinrich. *Theology and Preaching*. Translated by Harold Knight. Philadelphia: Westminster, 1965.

Placher, William C. *The Domestication of Transcendence: How Modern Thinking about God Went Wrong*. Louisville: Westminster John Knox, 1996.

Pope Francis. *The Joy of the Gospel*. New York: Image, 2013.

Preaching the Mystery of Faith: The Sunday Homily. United States Conference of Catholic Bishops, Washington, DC, 2012.

Ramshaw, Gail. *Christian Worship: 100,000 Sundays of Symbols and Rituals*. Minneapolis: Fortress, 2009.

_____. *A Three-Year Banquet: The Lectionary for the Assembly*. Minneapolis: Augsburg Fortress, 2004.

_____. *The Three-Day Feast: Maundy Thursday, Good Friday, Easter*. Minneapolis: Augsburg Fortress, 2004.

Rice, Charles L. *The Embodied Word: Preaching as Art and Liturgy*. Minneapolis: Augsburg Fortress, 1991.

Saliers, Don E. *Worship as Theology: Foretaste of the Glory Divine.* Nashville: Abingdon, 1994.

_____. *Worship Come to Its Senses.* Nashville: Abingdon, 1996.

Schleiermacher, Friedrich. *On Religion: Speeches to Its Cultured Despisers.* Edited by Richard Crouter. Cambridge: Cambridge University Press, 1996.

Senn, Frank C. *Christian Liturgy: Catholic and Evangelical.* Minneapolis: Fortress, 1997.

Skudlarek, William. *The Word in Worship: Preaching in a Liturgical Context.* Nashville: Abingdon, 1981.

Standish, N. Graham. *In God's Presence: Encountering, Experiencing, and Embracing the Holy in Worship.* The Alban Institute, 2010.

Stevick, Daniel B. *The Crafting of Liturgy.* New York: The Church Hymnal Corporation, 1990.

Stookey, Laurence Hull. *Baptism: Christ's Act in the Church.* Nashville: Abingdon, 1982.

_____. *Eucharist: Christ's Feast with the Church.* Nashville: Abingdon, 1993.

Taylor, Barbara Brown. *Bread of Angels.* Cambridge, MA: Cowley, 1993.

_____. "Foreword." In Fred B. Craddock, *Cherry Log Sermons.* Louisville: Westminster John Knox, 2004.

_____. *God in Pain: Teaching Sermons on Suffering.* Nashville: Abingdon, 1998.

_____. *Gospel Medicine.* Cambridge, MA: Cowley, 1995.

_____. "Preaching the Body." In *Listening to the Word: Studies in Honor of Fred B. Craddock,* ed. Gail R. O'Day and Thomas G. Long, 207–22. Nashville: Abingdon, 2003.

_____. *The Preaching Life.* Cambridge, MA: Cowley, 1993.

Thompson, Bard D., ed. *Liturgies of the Western Church.* New York: World, 1961; Minneapolis: Fortress, 1980 (reprint); Martino Fine Books, 2015 (reprint).

Thulin, Richard L. *The "I" of the Sermon.* Minneapolis: Augsburg Fortress, 1989.

Thurian, Max. *The Mystery of the Eucharist: An Ecumenical Approach.* Translated by Emily Chisholm. Grand Rapids: Eerdmans, 1981.

Thurian, Max, and Geoffrey Wainwright. *Baptism and Eucharist: Ecumenical Convergence in Celebration* (Faith and Order Paper No. 117). Geneva: World Council of Churches, 1983.

Tisdale, Leonora Tubbs. *Preaching as Local Theology and Folk Art.* Minneapolis: Fortress, 1997.

Troeger, Thomas H. "Coordinating with the Rest of the Service." In *Best Advice for Preaching*, ed. John S. McClure. Minneapolis: Fortress, 1998.

_____. *Imagining a Sermon*. Nashville: Abingdon, 1990.

_____. *The Parable of Ten Preachers*. Nashville: Abingdon, 1992.

Vajta, Vilmos. *Luther on Worship: An Interpretation*. Philadelphia: Muhlenberg, 1958.

Van Dyk, Leanne, ed. *A More Profound Alleluia: Theology and Worship in Harmony*. Grand Rapids: Eerdmans, 2005.

Wainwright, Geoffrey. *Doxology: The Praise of God in Worship, Doctrine, and Life*. New York: Oxford University Press, 1980.

Wainright, Geoffrey, and Karen B. Westerfield Tucker, eds. *The Oxford History of Christian Worship*. New York: Oxford University Press, 2006.

Wardlaw, Don M., ed. *Preaching Biblically: Creating Sermons in the Shape of Scripture*. Philadelphia: Westminster, 1983.

Webber, Robert E. *Ancient-Future Worship: Proclaiming and Enacting God's Narrative*. Grand Rapids: Baker, 2008.

Welker, Michael. *What Happens in Holy Communion?* Translated by John F. Hoffmeyer. Grand Rapids: Eerdmans, 2000.

Wengert, Timothy J., ed. *Centripetal Worship: The Evangelical Heart of Lutheran Worship*. Minneapolis: Augsburg Fortress, 2007.

Westermeyer, Paul. *The Church Musician*. San Francisco: Harper & Row, 1988.

White, James F. "A Protestant Worship Manifesto." *The Christian Century*, January 27, 1982.

_____. *Christian Worship in Transition*. Nashville: Abingdon, 1976.

_____. *Introduction to Christian Worship*. Nashville: Abingdon, 1980.

_____. *New Forms of Worship*. Nashville: Abingdon, 1971.

_____. *Protestant Worship: Tradition in Transition*. Louisville: Westminster John Knox, 1989.

_____. *Sacraments as God's Self-Giving*. Nashville: Abingdon, 1983, 2001.

_____. *The Sacraments in Protestant Practice and Faith*. Nashville: Abingdon, 1999.

Wilkey, Gláucia Vasconcelos. *Worship and Culture: Foreign Country or Homeland?* Grand Rapids: Eerdmans, 2014.

Willimon, William H. *The Intrusive Word: Preaching to the Unbaptized*. Grand Rapids: Eerdmans, 1994.

_____, and Richard Lischer, eds. *Concise Encyclopedia of Preaching*. Louisville: Westminster John Knox, 1995.

Wilson, Paul Scott. *A Concise History of Preaching*. Nashville: Abingdon, 1992.

_____. *God Sense: Reading the Bible for Preaching.* Nashville: Abingdon, 2001.

_____. *Imagination of the Heart: New Understandings in Preaching.* Nashville: Abingdon, 1988.

_____. *The Practice of Preaching.* Nashville: Abingdon, 1995.

Wilson-Kastner, Patricia. *Imagery for Preaching.* Minneapolis: Fortress, 1989.

Index

Index